When the Pipirite Sings

JEAN MÉTELLUS

When the Pipirite Sings

SELECTED POEMS

Translated by Haun Saussy

Northwestern University Press
Evanston, Illinois

Northwestern University Press
www.nupress.northwestern.edu

Printed in the United States of America

10 9 8 7 6 5 4 3 2 1

Library of Congress Cataloging-in-Publication Data
Names: Métellus, Jean, 1937–2014, author. | Saussy, Haun, 1960– translator.
Title: When the pipirite sings : selected poems / Jean Metellus ; translated
    from the French by Haun Saussy.
Other titles: Au pipirite chantant. English
Description: Evanston, Illinois : Northwestern University Press, 2019. |
    Includes bibliographical references.
Identifiers: LCCN 2018046657 | ISBN 9780810139787 (alk. paper) | ISBN
    9780810139794 (ebook)
Classification: LCC PQ2673.E7244 A913 2019 | DDC 841.914—dc23
LC record available at https://lccn.loc.gov/2018046657

CONTENTS

Naming the Lwas in a Paris Suburb

A Portrait of the Artist as Horse

Jean Métellus was born in 1937 in the once-prosperous coffee port of Jacmel on Haiti's southern coast, where his parents ran a bakery. (The aroma of fresh bread saturates his 1999 novel *L'Archevêque*.) After the consolidation of power by President-for-Life François Duvalier, he chose to study in France in 1959. There he studied linguistics and neurology, taking first an M.D. and then a Ph.D. with a thesis on the effects of degenerative nervous syndromes on speech, and joined the neurology staff of one of the large public hospitals outside Paris. Words and images stocked up in his mind began to pour out, mostly at night, in long and short poems reviving his memories of life in Haiti, a place that he never expected to see again as long as the Duvalier family dictatorship (1957–86) lasted. The long poem "Au pipirite chantant" (When the pipirite sings), the focus of the present collection, is a nearly hallucinatory evocation of the Haitian countryside, its subsistence farmers, wildlife, vegetation, and ineradicable population of West African–derived gods, the *lwas*. Formally and thematically, it has many ties to Aimé Césaire's *Notebook of a Return to the Native Land* (1939), which has deservedly taken a high place in the canon of French-language postcolonial writings.

Maurice Nadeau, a great discoverer of talent, published Métellus in his journal *Les lettres nouvelles* and then brought out his first book of poems, *Au pipirite chantant* (1978). A plentiful literary production continued until Métellus's death in 2014. He published novels, some about the Haiti of his youth (*Jacmel au crépuscule, La famille Vortex, L'année Dessalines, L'Archevêque*), some about earlier Haitian history (*Les Cacos*), and some, for the sake of exoticism, about such subjects as a retired Parisian doctor (*Charles-Honoré*

Bonnefoy) and residents of a Swiss village (*Une eau-forte*). *La famille Vortex* has been published in English translation under the title *The Vortex Family*. His play *Anacaona*, about the last Indian queen of the island of Santo Domingo, was staged by Antoine Vitez at the National Theater of Chaillot. His non-fiction writing included reflections on Haitian history and politics (*Haïti, une nation pathétique*; *Toussaint Louverture le précurseur*), on the iconography of slave emancipation (*De l'esclavage aux abolitions*), and a study of dyslexia in relation to creativity (*Vive la dyslexie!*, written with Béatrice Sauvageot). And he continued to write poetry: evocations of Haiti, commemorative odes on figures of the worldwide black struggle for equality, fugitive observations from daily life. The second career of Dr. Métellus was rewarded by major literary prizes: the Léopold Sédar Senghor Prize for French-Language Poetry in 2006, the Grand Poetry Prize of the Society of Writers in 2007, and the Benjamin Fondane International Prize in Francophone Poetry in 2010, among others.[1]

Jean Métellus has received some scholarly attention, but his unusual place as an exile writing about a remembered Haiti and his choice of French rather than Kreyòl as his language of expression make it tricky to insert him among the categories of *francophonie* and postcoloniality. Many Caribbean and African writers who, like him, reside abroad write in French, a decision that may be seen as turning their backs on their places of origin; not even the militancy of a Césaire was able to remove all such suspicion.[2] Métellus's public stances on Haitian politics were often discordant with the views of fellow exiles and of the relevant great powers (France, the United States, the United Nations), and his commemorations of black liberation figures sometimes encountered a chilly response in France, where race is a subject usually avoided. Since his death, his French publisher has brought out a collection of his essays on art, literature, history, and politics (*Jean Métellus et le miroir du monde*) and a retrospective poetry anthology (*Haïti, mon île exposée et secrète*) with a CD of well-known actors voicing his lines. This collection seeks to make his poems better known in the English-speaking world.

The Haitian writers of Métellus's generation, exiled or mistreated by the Duvalier kleptocracy—Marie Vieux-Chauvet, Jacques-Stéphen Alexis, René Depestre, René Bélance—wrote, like Métellus, almost exclusively in French, not Kreyòl. Yet I have often felt that I am the second translator of a work that began as the French version of a nonexistent Kreyòl original. It is not simply that Métellus sometimes uses vernacular Haitian terms and images—it is not a matter of local color—nor is it a linguistic distortion in the French, as if Métellus's sentences were shaped on a pattern from another language. Rather, it has to do with the poems' role as mediations and re-creations, their place in an act of giving voice. And this in turn derives from a history of indirect representation that defines Haitians' relation to one another and to the rest of the world, a history indivisible from the choice of a language in which to make those relations happen.

Ever since the physician, diplomat, and ethnographer Jean Price-Mars scolded the Haitian elite for their "collective Bovarysme," their "ability to imagine themselves otherwise than as they are," the existence of a copious Haitian literature in French has looked like a paradox.[3] (Haitian Kreyòl first attained the status of an official language in its home country in 1987.) Haitians had written, of course, and memorably, since before the founding of the independent Haitian Republic in 1804, but in the nineteenth century their language and references were chiefly "metropolitan"—that is, French.[4] Addressing French literary culture on a footing of equality, but nonetheless on French terms, was the goal of Haitian litterateurs, and understandably so, since Haiti's educational system with its promise of social promotion dispensed its favors in French. A national literature for Haitians began with the "slap" of American occupation in 1915, which awoke the elite from their dream of belonging to a European cultural cosmopolis. For Price-Mars and for the subsequent Indigenist and Negritude movements, the slap, however traumatic, set them on the path to self-recognition: "To the degree that we strove to believe in our status as 'colored' Frenchmen, we had forgotten how to be Haitians, that is, men born into determinate historical conditions."[5] Recently J. Michael Dash has expressed impatience with this normative, reductive account of national consciousness; he would make "displacement" the leitmotif of a literature, often written from exile, that connects such predecessors as Émile Nau (1812–1860) and Anténor Firmin (1856–1911) to our contemporaries Dany Laferrière and Edwidge Danticat.[6] Thus Haitian diglossia—formed primarily around the dyad of French and Kreyòl but including Kreyòl-English and Kreyòl-Spanish interactions—would reflect the divisions within Haitian literary culture. Like many older diglossias, Haitian literature flouts the Wilsonian assumption of a necessary identity of language, people, and nation.[7]

We think that we are born with a "native language," a "mother tongue"—an assumption belied by the experience of many people around the world who perform some of their acts in one language, some in another. And we assume that our personalities, however modified by experience, grow out of something we are born with, a singular self. The lyric poet condenses these expectations: not only do we often hear that it is impossible to write poetry in a language not one's own but also the poet is supposed to write from an intimate place of personal consciousness. Something of these assumptions about authenticity rise to the surface as Jean Jonassaint describes Jean Métellus as a difficult interview subject, recounting his frustration on two occasions when "each time the tension mounted, imperceptibly, with both of us defending a scrap of territory and trying to trap the other . . . The man is taciturn, *secret*, as little open as his texts are overflowing with emphasis."[8] The last phrase gives away Jonassaint's game. He must have thought that by interviewing Métellus he would be permitted to step close to the sonorous source of an overwhelming lyric bombardment, and thus he read the flesh-and-blood Métellus, who was not conspicuously like that, as wearing a mask, mounting a defense. But it may be that Métellus had nothing to hide. Asked about his writings, he preferred to speak of outward evidence rather than personal experience, of influences, circumstances, and publication dates rather than the processes that led up to them. Métellus was, to be sure, uneasy with the prying and lionizing that come with renown and wary of journalists' and critics' professional eagerness to go beyond or behind the works that he produced in the night hours. But his reluctance to answer questions about the motives of his writing seems less a rejection of the questions asked than of the appropriateness of asking *him*. The person whose name is on the title page may indeed not have known, or wanted to know, how novels and poems with the felicity and exactitude of *Jacmel au crépuscule* or *Au pipirite chantant* came about.

So profound a lack of curiosity may seem uncharacteristic of a man who otherwise showed himself to be on the most intimate terms with the analyzing and explaining intellect: consider his doctoral thesis on linguistic disorders, his work as a neurologist, his publications on dyslexia and aphasia. Well, then, what if the real author of Métellus's books were (not to be too specific) *someone else*?

In narrating his life, Métellus often insisted on the chancy, circumstantial nature of this or that life-changing decision. Métellus shared a hometown with many poets (including René Depestre, his senior by eleven years), but showed no particular youthful bent toward literature. After graduating from the École Normale Supérieure in Port-au-Prince he was appointed mathematics teacher at the venerable Lycée Pinchinat of Jacmel at the age of twenty. He taught for two years, joined the nascent and struggling National Secondary School Teachers' Union (becoming its regional spokesman), and then left Haiti "on account of what I felt was a climate of insecurity" in 1959.[9] The teachers' union was not particularly dear to the heart of François Duvalier (better known as Haiti's long-term dictator Papa Doc, first called to the presidency by election in 1957), and its representatives had to face much "crushing and breaking," as the saying went. Métellus's first idea had been to go to Spain, "a country where there was no democracy, of course, but living expenses weren't too high." But while passing through Paris he ran into friends, who persuaded him to stay and study for the French medical entrance exams. "So I came here and stayed on in Paris by accident . . . I had no idea where I was going, I was practically unaware of what I was doing . . . I didn't have a penny. The generosity of friends kept me alive. As a former teacher, I received some checks from the Haitian government during my first year of medical school . . . I had a single suit of clothes I wore year-round. But I passed the entrance exam even under those very difficult conditions." A job in the library of the Swiss Foundation of the University of Paris enabled him to spend whatever time he had left over from his medical studies reading. "I read Lorca, René Char, Aragon. I read a great deal of Balzac, one of my favorite novelists. And Tristan Tzara, and Breton." Three or four years into his medical training, he began writing little poems, "just like that. And before I knew it I couldn't stop. So I wrote a lot, quite a lot. And when I showed [Maurice] Nadeau what I had done up to then, he said, 'Fine, I'll publish you.'" These early poems appeared in *Les lettres nouvelles*, the review edited by Nadeau, during the middle and late sixties. Others followed, in publications such as *Présence africaine* and *Les temps modernes*. In the meantime their author had taken his degree and was working full-time as a neurologist in a Paris hospital. Did medicine and poetry meet for him on some common ground of metaphor, as they had for William Carlos Williams? "I have the impression of living two parallel lives. [Medicine] doesn't enter into my poetry."

The responsibilities of the clinic and the hours consecrated to literature early every morning did not keep Métellus from research into the pathology of language. Curiously, that research (which resulted in 1975 in a Ph.D. in linguistics at the Sorbonne) had much to do with his training as a neurologist and almost nothing to do with the way the poet in him handled language.[10] "I don't think I would have gone to linguistics if I weren't already in neurology. It's because we know a little about the structures of language in the brain that I wanted to do some linguistics, in order to try to compare what we neurologists know about the brain and what linguistics, for its part, helps us to understand . . . But between those two disciplines and my writing career—no connection."

Au pipirite chantant was the first of Métellus's writings to reach publication in book form. Even with its tremendous title poem, it is only a pebble removed from "a mountain of poems," as he matter-of-factly put it. It is a vivid re-creation of Haiti as perhaps only expatriates can see it. "La mort à Haïti" (Death in Haiti) voices nostalgia and lament from abroad:

> Nowhere will a living creature be better received.
> Nowhere do the Cyclones, Storms, and Tempests find a better terrain, better exert their power, sing more loudly, carry off more children in their arms, find so many shacks or so much life to fill up the waters rolling night and day.
> . . .
> Nowhere in the world is the child more fragile, the mother more burdened.
> Nowhere in the world do the jaws of the earth find fresher meat.
> Nowhere do the graveyards suck up more children.
>
> Nulle part vivant ne peut être mieux reçu.
> Nulle part Cyclones, Orages, Tempêtes ne trouvent meilleur terrain, ne déploient mieux leur force, ne chantent plus fort, n'entraînent plus d'enfants dans leurs bras, ne trouvent tant de cabanes, de vie pour occuper les eaux qui roulent tout le jour, toute la nuit.
> . . .
> Nulle part dans le monde l'enfant n'est plus fragile la mère plus accablée.
> Nulle part dans le monde les crocs de la terre ne trouvent de chair plus fraîche.
> Nulle part les cimetières n'aspirent plus d'enfants.[11]

Exile of some form or duration has been practically inescapable for Haitian writers of the past fifty years or so. A representative career is that of Métellus's older contemporary René Depestre, shuttling around France, Eastern Europe, Cuba, and France again since his forced departure from Haiti in 1946 for political activism. Métellus is a special case in that he discovered a need to write poetry some years after leaving Haiti, while most of the others began their wanderings already conscious of their talent and usually with publications to their credit. (These, of course, were not infrequently the reason for their having to become expatriates.) "They were already poets. But as for me . . . well, let's say it took possession of me [ça m'a chevauché] while I was abroad." Métellus described his compositional process to me as a long gestation period in which every detail of the future work is thought out before pen ever touches paper. In this sense it could be argued that the poems of *Au pipirite chantant* were already being composed, in the form of memory and observation, during Métellus's childhood and youth in Jacmel. "When you've been Haitian for twenty-two years, you can't forget it . . . I have only to close my eyes to see Jacmel, the streets, and all that. Maybe they've changed since. I always see the landscapes I grew up in." Taught to read and write in French, not Kreyòl, Métellus was skeptical of his ability to do justice to Kreyòl as a literary language.

To respond, however belatedly, to Jonassaint: the difficulty of interviewing Métellus may have been that there were simply so many parallel lives to the man, lives among which he refused to draw analogies or chart influences. But those were not the only mechanisms that he declined to investigate. Asked about his unusual road from exile to writing (instead of the inverse), his answer was as follows:

> There probably is a link between exile and the fact that I write,
> but I don't have any theoretical opinion on the question. I only
> have a theoretical opinion on my specialties, neurology and
> linguistics; on everything else I have no opinion. People form
> opinions easily, and when you look into them you often find
> that—well, linguistics and neurology have taught me that there is
> such a thing as language without thought—that is, often people
> talk without having anything to say. They don't know what they
> mean, but they say it anyway . . . I want to avoid that. So: I don't
> make theories.[12]

The conclusion looms that his own writing was not one of Métellus's "specialties": something he could not have an opinion on except to "talk without having anything to say." And for this reason interviews with the author tended to stall, or had to be shifted to some other topic—Haiti, Toussaint Louverture, painting, the history of psychiatry. The final impression was that if the man Métellus was there, the poet was out, and visitors went away feeling that they had not encountered what they had hoped to see.

Why is this? It may be that Métellus, far from trying to "pull rank on the critics" (as Jonassaint puts it), was simply unable to account for the poems he left his clinic, his classroom, and his family every day to write.[13]

A commonsense explanation, which the reader is not obliged to accept, is simply that Métellus carried three or four souls in the same body, that the neurologist, the private man, the imaginative writer, and the author of studies in linguistic psychology each had no way of knowing what the others were up to, except when the coincidences of a common language made comparisons possible. But that is not the same as saying that "Métellus"—the signature appended to all this—could easily travel between the different faces of his achievement. Rather, we can imagine that the doctor stumbled on articles by the cognitive linguist that suggested new approaches to him, or the other way around; but neither of them, apparently, read poetry.

Another way of putting this is to suggest that his poetic vein was a form of possession. How else indeed to account for Métellus's phenomenal production and energy? Alfred Métraux makes the following observations about subjects of possession by the lwa of Haitian *vaudou*:

> A lwa enters the head of an individual after chasing away the "big guardian angel," one of the two souls that inhabit every person . . . Once the "guardian angel" has left, the person possessed has a feeling of utter emptiness, as in fainting . . . He then becomes not only the receptacle of a god but also the god's instrument. The god's personality, not his own, finds expression in his behavior and speech . . . The rapport uniting the lwa and the man seized by him is often compared to that between a rider and a horse.

And so, precisely, does Métellus describe poetry's "straddling" him in his third year of medical school: *ça m'a chevauché*.

The nature of the crisis [of possession] varies according to the character of the spirit that seeks to be embodied. Mighty and terrible lwa enter their fleshly disguise with a hurricane's violence . . . On emerging from the trance the possessed person claims to have no memory of anything he did or said in that state . . . It is expected that no one should know that he has been a spirit's dwelling place, unless he learns it from someone else.[14]

Among the deprivations of exile, Métellus mentioned regretting "that I was never able to spend enough time around *vaudou* temples to be initiated, and to find out for myself what possession is."[15] Reading Métellus, one begins to think that for an amateur he did very well indeed. With the lurid vigor of his imagery, the license every one of his sentences has to run away with a poem or an episode, his fusion of lyrical and epic modes, Métellus in *Au pipirite chantant* is of the same stuff as Blake in his prophetic books. Just as, in some sects of *vaudou*, possession takes precedence over all other ritual observances (sacrifice, prayer, healing, and so forth), so in Métellus the great metaphors of weather and landscape, power and destruction, vegetation and astronomy build up into an intensely imagined private religion. (So private, indeed, that the neighboring souls of its author were not even communicants.) And sooner or later all those metaphors prove to be allegorical of the poetic inspiration that brings them to the *houmfò*, or shrine, of the printed page.

Each lwa has a characteristic language and field of competence. Polytheism tends to specialize. That Ogoun, originally a Nago (Yoruba) war god captured and worked into the Dahomey pantheon, should be the main speaker of poems in which present-day Haitians are scolded for having forgotten the spirits who helped them overthrow the slave regime ("Ogoun") is understandable enough. The long poem "When the Pipirite Sings," described by its author as a "song to the glory of the Haitian peasant," is a verbal Jacob's ladder with messengers ascending and descending on it. It includes addresses to and from a variety of gods, among them the sun and a variety of tree, the *mapou*, in which wandering spirits are reported to dwell. The sea god Agoué appropriately introduces a meditation on the geographical and cultural displacement of New World Africans; Ogoun appears briefly, smoking; the sun's speech aims at the philosophical comprehensiveness of the *Bhagavad-Gita*; and sections of the poem are written in the poetic mode corresponding to the countrified Zakas. (Métraux again: "Fields and field labor are the domain of the lwa Zaka, who is 'Minister of Agriculture' in the divine world . . . When the Zakas take a believer's human shape, they always dress like country people in straw hat and denim shirt, with a rope bag slung over one shoulder and stubby pipe between the teeth.")[16]

But while Métellus's poetry is split up among many recognizable speakers, in another sense it is all one poem: for instance, segments of "To a Haitian Schoolboy" filter into "When the Pipirite Sings," and "No Reprieve," seemingly complete in *Au pipirite chantant*, gains in *Voyance* an appendix three times as long as the original poem. Like an oral text—which is not to say that there is anything primitive or preliterate about it—the written poem or play in Métellus's oeuvre is only one realization of a theme or memory locus that can always be revisited.[17] The positions or perspectives arrived at in one writing come back on other occasions, not because they are fixed and definitive but rather because the confrontation with new situations can still renew them. Just as the daily drama of possession and release in every functioning *houmfô* grows out of the traditional cast of characters whose improvised running soap opera is available, in countless variations, all over Haiti, so the new poem partly coinciding with pieces of old poems personifies the already written lines: it enlists them as participants in a conversational riff. (Depestre's "voodoo mystery poem" *A Rainbow for the Christian West* harnesses the stock characters of folk religion for similar innovative uses.)[18]

To unite the neurologist, the linguist, and the poet in Métellus, one could do worse than to start from the category of personality, with all its divisions and multiplications and interferences. Métellus's insistence that he has no personal opinions, that the writer in him is straddled by the spiritual forces that direct the poem, familiar though it all looks, is something quite different from the cult of inspiration—Plato's poetic "madness"—that makes us look on poets as beings apart. Plato's Socrates tried to hem in poetic madness because he feared its demagogic power: the speaker whom the gods possessed might, in turn, possess his hearers and induce them to accept his fictions as the truth.[19] But for Métellus the determination to avoid saying too much in his own name corresponds to an aversion of conscience provoked by what he sees as a fatal penchant for political logorrhea in his country: "language without thought." (A similar fastidiousness about language inspired René Bélance to write in a way that would "mute eloquence.")[20] Commenting on one of his novels, Métellus used a curious passive construction:

Who are the people who talk in this book [*Jacmel au crépuscule*]? There's not a single peasant, not a single worker, who speaks in the book—other people talk about them. I wanted to show that these people, [characters like] Maître Barthoux and Jean-Philippe Murat, talk a lot; they have an explanation for everything. Well, they talk the country. The country *gets talked.* The peasants get talked, the workers get talked, they never speak for themselves . . . I wanted to show by this that those who talk demand silence from the rest.[21]

The loss of personality implicit in "getting talked" is nowhere imagined more vividly or more extremely than in the Haitian folklore of zombification.

On this soil which turned the race of its children to smoke
Among the bullets which perforated your body and charred your birth
    certificate
You imagined a nighttime census bureau, one whose registry office
    would be lodged in the cemetery.
On this accursed soil of Hispaniola, you conceived a new creature: the
    man with no needs, no cares, well adjusted at last
Black man, you alone had the secret of the zombies
    You sculpted a world in the shadows of refusal.

Sur cette terre qui a fumé la race de ses enfants
Devant ces balles qui ajouraient ton corps et brûlaient ton acte de
    naissance
Il t'est venu l'idée d'un état civil qui fonctionnerait la nuit, qui aurait son
    registre au cimetière
Sur cette terre maudite d'Hispianola, tu as conçu une nouvelle créature:
    l'homme sans besoin, sans souci, enfin sensé
O nègre, toi seul avais le secret des Zombis
    Tu as sculpté un monde dans les ténèbres du refus.[22]

Zombification was for Métellus the condensed image of Haiti's history and sufferings—not to mention its literature. Literature is part of the problem so long as the stratification of languages (French for the few, Kreyòl for the many) and the difficulty for most people of accessing education or public platforms make it easy for litterateurs to do others' talking for them. Writing that is irresponsible, self-promoting, or based on false premises of spokesmanship only extends the work of zombification. "You could apply words like 'politically engaged' to my work, but 'engagement' is far more difficult for someone actually writing in Haiti. Here on the outside, it's too easy to declaim 'Down with this, down with that.'"

In spirit possession, too, the peasant's body "gets talked" by the gods and spirits, but the result is release and compensation. (Perhaps because the gods, wanting nothing more than to appear, need the devotee's help?) A comprehensive understanding of *vaudou* speech in its social contexts is probably necessary to deciphering Métellus's modes of language: talking, the silence that comes of "getting talked," and the heightened speech of the *houmfô*. It comes as no surprise that Métellus's favorite and most-reread author is Shakespeare, the writer with an imagination so rich he could afford to give it all away and appear, in his "negative capability," to be "nothing in himself, but all that others were, or that they could become."[23]

If Métellus's lyric poems tend to grow into the proportions and perspectives of epics—see "Ogoun," for example—it is the myths of Haitian history that provide the middle ground. He returned repeatedly to the essential scenes and personalities: the African gods; Anacaona, the last queen of Haiti's original Taino inhabitants; Toussaint and Christophe. Most unusually for a Caribbean writer, Métellus saw in Christopher Columbus more than the originator of genocide, more than an import-export Faust figure. "There is much about Columbus to detest, but also a lot that is admirable as well. You'd have to be daring to do what he did, and it's that aspect of his life, the strength and clairvoyance, that I pay homage to, not the power-hungry side." In *Hommes de plein vent*, a book of poems dominated by history and biography, Columbus takes his place alongside the martyred black intellectuals Malcolm X and Jacques-Stéphen Alexis.

A writer far from his original setting must have some complex relation to the different worlds among which he or she circulates. What was Métellus's attitude, I wanted to know, toward the literary politics of the generations that preceded him, the contrary pulls toward "indigenism" and "universalism" that led Haitian writers at times to emphasize their kinship with French, Latin American, or African traditions and at other times to delve into the ethnology and folklore of their homeland for authentic subject matter and form?

I think that's all in the past now. The housecleaning's been done and the rooms are in order . . . Now I don't just demand the right to say who I am, but the right to talk about anything, anywhere . . . Which is one of the reasons why I set [*Une eau-forte*] in Switzerland. The characters in that book are Europeans, Swiss people: it's strictly a problem of imagination, and I see no reason why I shouldn't be allowed to invent Europeans . . . I owe this to the *négritude* movement. The battle's won . . . It would have been unthinkable in 1920 for a black man to write what I wrote in 1982–1983. People would have rejected it instantly—whereas Europeans could visit Haiti, spend a week on the beach, and come back with a novel about life in the countryside!

In a way it is the proof of the *indigéniste* movement's success that its inheritors can now dispense with the outward forms of "local color" that had been its theme and its pride. Identity movements can be self-limiting. "When the Pipirite Sings," that hymn to the Haitian farmer, closes with a boast that

> . . . what I say, bound up with my source, gags the foaming of all
> extrinsic waters—all decorous cries—and shod in irreverence tramples
> the hubbub of all foreign words

> . . . mon propos, lié à ma source, bâillonne l'écume de toutes les eaux
> étrangères, de tous les cris de convenance et chausse l'irrévérence
> pour fouler le brouhaha de tous les mots d'ailleurs

But it takes a reading of the poem to know what inflection to put on the word "foreign." Métellus's speaker is more concerned to chase timidity and decorum than any national or extranational literary tradition (even the prime suspect, the dominating French influence). In the biographical poems it is always "words" that buzz around the hero to perplex or redeem him; and no poet makes words more animate than Métellus. Whatever its author may claim to have forgotten or never known, Métellus's poetry exemplifies the tireless memory (memory for words and memory for things) personified, also near the end of "Au pipirite chantant," in an allegory cast from the same metal as Homer's "Prayers" and "Ruin":

And memory dressed in stars still signs with a flourish across the wound
    of oblivion
Intrepid she rushes to all fronts, reviving despair

Et la mémoire tout habillée d'étoiles laisse encore traîner son paraphe
    sur la blessure de l'oubli
Intrépide elle va au trot sur tous les fronts raviver la désespérance

For there are also the spirits of Prayer, the daughters of great Zeus,
and they are lame of their feet, and wrinkled, and cast their eyes
    sidelong,
who toil on their way left far behind by the spirit of Ruin:
but she, Ruin, is strong and sound on her feet, and therefore
she outruns all Prayers, and wins into every country
to force men astray; and the Prayers follow as healers after her.

(Homer, *Iliad* 9.502–7)[24]

Whether or not his writing emerged from actual states of possession, Métellus offered himself as a "horse" to speed the mercies of Haitian memory. His vocalization or ventriloquism comprehends several modes of allegory or other-speech: the *vaudou* gods' possession of the worshippers, the literate person's speaking for the peasant, the French language's function as the Foreign Affairs Section of Kreyòl, the remembered landscape speaking through the remembering brain. These transformations make up the substance of Métellus's one big poem, the discovery of which was his nightly task. Translatedness is its authenticity, and other translators merely extend the process.

Notes

1. Ginette Adamson, "Jean Métellus: Insuffler une respiration jacmélienne à la mémoire haïtienne," in *Écrits d'Haïti: Perspectives sur la littérature haïtienne contemporaine (1986–2006)*, ed. Nadève Menard, 39–48 (Paris: Karthala, 2011); "Le poète et neuro-linguiste haïtien Jean Métellus est mort," *L'Humanité,* January 6, 2014; Jean-Michel Caroit, "Jean Métellus (1937–2014), figure de la scène intellectuelle haïtienne," *Le Monde,* January 15, 2014.

2. See Carrie Noland, "Red Front / Black Front: Aimé Césaire and the Affaire Aragon," *Diacritics* 36, no. 1 (2006): 64–84.

3. Jean Price-Mars, *Ainsi parla l'Oncle: essais d'ethnographie* (Thus spake the Uncle: Ethnographic essays) (Port-au-Prince: Chenet, 1928), reprinted in *Ainsi parla*

l'Oncle suivi de Revisiter l'Oncle (Thus spake the Uncle, followed by Revisiting the Uncle) (Montreal: Mémoire d'encrier, 2009), 8. Price-Mars's first effort to define Haitian national identity as multiple yet interconnected was a series of talks delivered in the immediate aftermath of the U.S. invasion and published as *La vocation de l'élite* (The vocation of the elite) (Port-au-Prince: Chenet, 1919).

4. For an overview of Haitian writing from colonial times to the middle of the Duvalier period, see Raphaël Berrou and Pradel Pompilus, *Histoire de la littérature haïtienne illustrée par les textes*, 3 vols. (Port-au-Prince: Éditions Caraïbes, 1975–77). Stopping just at the moment of Métellus's entry onto the scene, this history provides indispensable background to the present work.

5. Price-Mars, *Ainsi parla l'Oncle: essais d'ethnographie*, 8; see also 202–4.

6. See the following by J. Michael Dash: "Nineteenth-Century Haiti and the Archipelago of the Americas: Anténor Firmin's Letters from St. Thomas," *Research in African Literatures* 35, no. 2 (2004): 44–53; "Fictions of Displacement: Locating Modern Haitian Narratives," *Small Axe* 27, no. 3 (2008): 32–41; "Haïti première république noire des lettres," April 21, 2011, http://actesbranly.revues.org/480.

7. For the classic formulation of divergence between "high" and "low" languages in a culture, see Charles A. Ferguson, "Diglossia," *Word* 15, no. 2 (1959): 325–40. For a long-term case of a high-culture language spreading across a wide and diverse area, see Sheldon Pollock, *The Language of the Gods in the World of Men: Sanskrit, Culture, and Power in Premodern India* (Berkeley: University of California Press, 2006). On the diglossia of Haiti's revolutionary hero Toussaint Louverture, see Philippe R. Girard, "Quelle langue parlait Toussaint Louverture? Le mémoire du fort de Joux et les origines du kreyòl haïtien," *Annales* 68, no. 1 (2013): 109–32.

8. Jean Jonassaint, *Le Pouvoir des mots, les mots du pouvoir* (Montreal: Presses de l'Université de Montréal, 1986), 218. Another volume of interviews, *Sous la dictée du vrai* (with Jacques-Hubert de Poncheville [Paris: Desclée de Brouwer, 1999]), gives an impression that is hardly more forthcoming.

9. Unattributed quotations are transcribed from conversations with Jean Métellus conducted by Paul Farmer (Paris, 1985) and Haun Saussy (Paris, 2001, 2002, 2004).

10. Métellus's dissertation was titled "Analyse linguistique de corpus de langage d'aphasiques" (A linguistic corpus analysis of aphasic utterances) (University of Paris III, 1975).

11. Jean Métellus, *Au pipirite chantant* (Paris: Les Lettres Nouvelles, 1978), 38.

12. Métellus, interview with Paul Farmer, Paris, 1985; see also Jean Métellus, "L'automatisme et la volonté dans le langage de l'aphasique âgé," *Médecine et hygiène* 35 (1977): 1961–65.

13. Jonassaint, *Le pouvoir des mots*, 218.

14. Alfred Métraux, *Le vaudou haïtien* (Paris: Gallimard, 1958), 106–8.

15. Jonassaint, *Le pouvoir des mots*, 227.

16. Métraux, *Le vaudou haïtien*, 95.

17. Métellus commemorated another explorer of oral literature in "Marcel Jousse et l'anthropologie du geste," *Nouvelle revue française* 332 (1980): 60–67.

18. René Depestre, *Un arc-en-ciel pour l'occident chrétien: Poème-mystère vaudou* (Paris: Présence Africaine, 1967), translated by Joan Dayan as *A Rainbow for the Christian West* (Amherst: University of Massachusetts Press, 1977).

19. Plato, *Republic*, 595a 1–608b 10.

20. Haun Saussy, "A Note on René Bélance" and "Fourteen Poems by René Bélance," *Callaloo* 22, no. 2 (1999): 351–62.

21. Jonassaint, *Le Pouvoir des mots*, 220–21. The parallel with Gramsci's analysis of cultural hegemony in prefascist Italy—also a stratified, nominally democratic society riven by regional, linguistic, and educational differences—is evident. See Thomas R. Bates, "Gramsci and the Theory of Hegemony," *Journal of the History of Ideas* 36, no. 2 (1975): 351–66.

22. "Les Zombis," in *Hommes de plein vent, hommes de plein ciel* (Paris: Éditions de Janus, 2011), 89–90.

23. John Keats, letter to George and Thomas Keats, December 22, 1817, in *The Complete Poetical Works and Letters of John Keats* (Boston: Houghton Mifflin, 1899), 277; William Hazlitt, "Shakespeare and Milton," in *Lectures on the English Poets* (Oxford: Oxford University Press, 1952), 70.

24. Richmond Lattimore, trans., *The Iliad of Homer* (Chicago: University of Chicago Press, 1951), 211.

When the Pipirite Sings

When the Pipirite Sings

When the pipirite sings the Haitian peasant has already crossed the day's
threshold and forms in the air, one step behind the sun, the outline of a
crucified man embracing life
Then blessing the earth with pure winds of devotion, first greets the
light-soaked azure and then drenches the forsaken hillside—no favor and
no fertilizer—with prayers
Around the pipirite's song hovers the threat of a return to tears
When the pipirite sings the hours dangle from the plantations' lips

And if yesterday came back what then

And the Haitian peasant morning after morning leaps across dawn's
tongue to slay the venom of his nights and crush his nightmares' thorns
And in the day's breath all the lwas are named

When the pipirite sings the Haitian peasant stands and breathes in light,
the scent of roots, palm trees' arrowshafts, the leafy dawn
He drives trouble from his body's every pore and plunges magic fingers in
the glebe
The Haitian peasant knows how to get up before dawn and bury a wish, a
dream
On purple-clad terraces he is seized by life, by coffee bushes' eyes, by the
cornstalks' manes feeding on heavenly fire
The Haitian peasant at pipirite song lifts a heel against night and goes to
whisper his troubles to the earth in one candle's flickering light

---

lwas: tutelary gods, often associated with a place, lineage, or individual

And his ear trusts vegetable patience sooner than the lust for great deeds,
    the weeds' insurrection over pulpit-born prowesses
For he slights memory and thinks up projects
He dismisses the past woven in scourges and smoke
And from daybreak on recites his glory upon fresh galleries of young shoots

Smack in the gods' face, inexhaustible balm bewitches the underbrush,
    murmurs in the creeks, takes root in the soil, babbles in the barnyard,
    roars in the ocean, spies on men, and makes the horizon blue
And the peasant curses fate sunk in night, flavorless days, tear-washed
    sleep, and a life all broken threads
When the pipirite sings the Haitian peasant shaves in pure spring water,
    cools his cheeks, and waits for the sun's caress
When the pipirite sings this prince of predawn dresses in innocence, takes
    the paths in hand, and blesses existence
And the lunge of his efforts exalts gardens crammed with seeds, with ears
    of grain, with human sweat

In the cooing of dawn
His lunatic wife, loud with dis-ease, importuned grace
Up before day in the shards of a dream
Hair loose, anxious nostrils groping at crumbs of life
Eyes hungry for signs
Ears alert, fearless, gauging the range of silence, exploring the hours'
    undertow and sensitive, in truth, to every volley of the waves
The mother, the mother got up and went around the house
Drunk, deprived of her smile and her sex, no leisure, no longings, she
    attacked the vapors of fear, bolts of solitude, pains that flourished at dawn
She mumbled, ironing, untangling a bad dream
And faith disguised with the tones of hell rose up in smoke columns,
    rubbed smooth, lost in her temples' estuary, puffed up by thirst
This was the beginning of her blasphemy
For a chipped word is a universe out of joint, a faded promise, an offended
    breast, a vanished pleasure, a soured yeast
For this mother, life was rising
Plundered memories, strata of restlessness, leapt from her famine,

And all mothers suffered together in a sumptuous plain among lizards,
    termite hills, ticks and ants
Before daybreak this mother was contemplating
Her womb more fertile than the earth
The shoots and pods of her body
Each moon tide's black blood
The volcanoes brought to life by her hips
This mother arrested life and upbraided it, counting the destruction of her
    joys
She stupefied faith
Her days massed into a pile of potsherds
Her efforts annoyed fate
Hell yapped in her fireplace
And who can accomplish hell's designs if not the demon himself
The devil raged
Hell's heiress sang
She soaked her pepper-laden mind in funereal fanfares
The demon made her pure and she turned demonic
For the sleep and bread of her sons
And the breadfruit tree addressed her, saying:

The bark of my vigor has grown thick

I am the island conqueror

Giant, generous

Decked out like rumpled hair

Like a stubborn crest

Studded with humors and prowesses

Wrapped in the very flesh of day

My foliage takes part in noonday rest

Pink entrails of the world's sobbing

Like a silent-pithed loaf

Plumed as a comet, I hear the evening discussions

And my antlers, my sapwood, my foot, and my tassel unravel tales,
complaints, stir the

impact of vision and reawaken dreams

My forehead measures the flight of every wish

For in all of them have I lodged my trembling song

And given my liveliest marrow to hunger's murmurs
Given brilliance to the body's sovereignty
My entranced shoulder delivers every virtue
My skin, my flesh, light
My grandeur and my crest
Rustic stem of summer, fronded and luxuriant peak
All set for revolution
Yes I say to the Caribbean's breath
I'll deal in violence
I'll cast laziness to the winds
Like the sun bathing the earth
Like prickles rasping a traveler's feet
Bare, winged, slender
On the day of great ceremonies I will be the bright path, clear and
vigilant sensuality, I will be wet like alert and swollen desire
I will protect the unreasonable, the disobedient, the angry, and the
rebellious
My fruits will descend bunch by bunch
Grains and drupes cluttering the glebe
I will be the rebel's arm and the beggar's sword
And over every man and every life will I spread the salacious odor
of great insurrections

When the pipirite sings every drop of dew, every trembling branch, the
    wind caressing the arbors, all are spirit messengers
When the pipirite sings sadness paints the heart
Even hope is sulfurous
The countryside reawakens its mysteries
Already stalking its dead
Its belly great with litters of trouble
The dead grow huge beneath the living
And the Haitian plain has received its splash of water
Spring water brought in by canal
Heaven's water like a roof of dew
Water from the eyes of a child without bread
Blood of a mother seized by madness

Color, taste, odor have flown under the cropper's long blade

The hollows' flanks yawn with fury
Arrows of silence slash signs and presages
The Haitian peasant hungers for a calm evening
His arm turns and bruises the furrows
His entrails have ravaged his dream hive
Gravel's mockery frightens his pace
And all grasses shiver
Now the coal is lit on his tongue and burns layers of his joy
Now dawn brandishes the eternal threat not to come again
And now in his brother's mouth a bush boils with insults, where the hours
    go and are burned to ashes
Reefs, wrecking hope
Through the feverish sole of his trance shudders the sorcerers' message
And his heart like a thirsty courser searches out rivers of health, feeds one
    spark of courage
And shakes out seeds right in the face of the wind
The *hounsis* have exhaled their oracles

When the pipirite sings everything moves in my head
I hang from a ripening fruit and from fields peopled by me
And my powers cut a spray of lunacies in the light
Which harass flowers in the distance
My rift swoops down on the breath of orchards
And anguish dances in the oasis of my soul
While everything, dressed in sadness, hums
Blotching my senses' aurora
Fanning unheard-of visions

What do you want from me, nightmare?
Shall I name you deliverance
You, marrow of my sorrows
Like a freedom-loving thorn
You always come alive at the juncture of my passions
Trudging alongside my breath
Suspended heavily there where I sleep

---

hounsis: attendants at a *vaudou* service

Woven into my nights my days
You've clung to my skin since I was born
You, little token of curly Africa
Sun torn by emotions
Laden with stars and torpor
You live in me more permanent than respiration
Taking your toll of my pleasures and songs
Diluting my games and joys
Twisting even the lightning of my dreams
And my bread is without savor
You live from my skin but you know nothing of metamorphosis
My moments of rest, tattered, pockmarked, sad and bare as an abandoned
    quarry
You'll never change and make me long to see strange lands
But let me spare my blood the cares of this world
And my skin, blisters and plagues
My helmet licked by your licentious tongue
My gloss masked by the gall of your veins
My prayers are born, grow old, sleepless, gazing into the candle
O sadness, Lord of the Tropics, you weave the light of my evenings with
    the bones of your ghosts, with the key of your secrets, with your tears
    and your sobs
And my palms sweat cries
As silence sweats restraint
With flowers and suffering
For a word I weaned long ago
Sadness, my childhood's fog
My fate's steel
You my patched face
My bony passion
My icy, broken skin
Spur and torment of my life
My dungeon, my jail
Where is the mild calm wind of my thoughts?
Anxiety creeps over my lips
Terror erupts
And I'm afraid of my own breathing
Iron like a flute makes my voice shudder

Iron rankles my recklessness
Iron fires my every move
The flight of days across my skin makes iron laugh
Iron cuts short my joy and my speech
And disrupts my path
In the heat of my own blood
In the odor of my own song
A man flogged by hope
A man with no past and no tomorrow
Like a spoiled cassava
Like an out-of-date salve
I am faceless
Like an embarrassed dream
Discomfited by life
Perplexed by my body
Isolated by fate
Dried out by death
A man fascinated by his own dark places
Bewitched by his own breath

Despair has no recollection
It awakens to shudders of silver
For despair, everything is dead and buried
Like the rainbow-hued wing of a dove
The flavorsome glow of harvest
A spring smiling up at the stars
The tender pearly cool of summer
Murmurs of obedient streams
Doleful moving meadows
Erosion at the setting of mercy

All pleasure belongs to the earth
The body takes the sufferings, says the despondent man

And the hiccup of a vacated body is a greater shudder than a falcon's
    swoop
Life trickles through the membranes of silence
The despondent man comes to enjoy his tears

The earth splits open, the wind howls, the lightning goes dark, the
    thunder growls,
Rain, storm, terror, the despondent man's prayer is answered
Calm, rootless, shielded by the shade
A remnant of space and time
A survivor of massacres, dumps, ruins
He sings in the catastrophe

Everything moves
And dies by breaking loose
And all is reborn suffused with noise
Chuffed along by the gins of sex
Daily death and resurrection
Erotic and mystical aquarium
Vertigo signifying mourning
This is the lascivious hygiene of the seasons
Satanic chromatism of the senses
Imperial alchemy of night
Savage formula of the dark
The hasty grain has fallen
Thrown, raw, stunned,
Muddy and prodigious
Ready and combed for a long rest
The traveler's attentiveness sowed it
Pallid, dull, straining the soil for the tree's greater glory
It drinks in dew
Rain comes and drags it elsewhere
The plain takes it in
And the grain sinks into the earth and exhales red magic
Its coat has burst
Awkward among earth's bedclothes
Alone in its mother's arms
Absorbing her juice, drinking her water
Robbed of its bloom, its inside
Barkless and shell-less
Ah the undertaking, to reinvent unity
To reproduce the seasons' spasm

Earth has opened for the seed
And bled for it
And forms two protective banks
    a new hull of life loaded with sentinels
    a passionate armor
    a defensive cloak
And the seed enlarges its dwelling
    stretches limbs out into its domain,
        adds to it
    forgets its whole past
And sprouts
And begets its mother
Earth dense with buds has delivered hope
Unleashed prayers climb skyward
Life's sessions circulate in the soil
And the tired mother invites hope to the ball of sun and water
For my children (says the earth) I drink all kinds of water
Spring water, sky water
Even the water of the body's depths
For my children (says the earth) I've drunk it all
And the high-belted *mapou*, capped with wind and birds, teases the alliance
    and celebrates the gods' memory
Lover of the unknown, its crest rides a starry thornbale
Darkness cooler than pink dawn, fuller than the sunflower's face, denser
    than drafts of new-mown grass, strong, vital, unreasonable as the sea's
    instinct, hangs harvest and offering on illusion's skirts
But hope, my soul's shoulder, roadbed of my nights
Hope tugs at anxiety's grasp and ripens on wounded shores
When the mapou grants an audience to less hardy trees
When water grows drunk on its voice
When the sun weighs its seasons
And the plain strips its bark
When the river mocks its debris
And silence conquers rhythm
Man settles his glory and triumph

———

mapou: a tall tree of the *Ficus* family native to Haiti with great significance in *vaudou*

And delivers his love to the snakes of time
And thunder takes possession of his words' empty hides
Like Satan's designated proxy
And the countryside, wondrous engulfer and giver of energy, but also
    dark asylum of specters and fear, domain of gullets and of the populace,
    washes its aprons in peasant tears
As the sun hangs its washing on the stars' scenery
As the river hatches waves of larvae on its banks
And the mapous' fabulous flummery blackens the summer's milky breath
Night entombs its densities and hides its veils
And day makes destinies to dance in their tunnel; it shakes out its claws
    and forces man to do battle
For the mapous had given counsel in the days of drought:
They made man lay his claim
They spoke against deforestation

When the pipirite sings it's with inspired hair
              with eyes bathed in hope
              with a nose that snuffles out the roots
that the peasant goes his way, his heart praising the smoke of a charcoal
    fire
He sows the desires of his ancestors
And the smiling boats of hope exult in my sight
But the hillsides' foreheads and the morning light re-create a garden of
    marvels and garner the truth of existence
And tireless I question on the margins of doubt
And I enumerate the quiverings of moons and stars
To shake loose the glory of those thrones that yawn over my sweat
To incinerate a gamut of thorns, ghosts, and caterpillars poised to teach
    death
Abruptly a spiderweb wrests the lwas' favor from me and makes the
    houmfort's pillars rock
When the pipirite sings my heart is in torment, my head mustered by the
    power of wishes
Good weather briefly glistens

------
houmfort: or *houmfò*, a *vaudou* temple

My fears burst like geysers in the hollow of oblivion, amid the sinkholes,
    the limestone, the boulders, and the echoes
Morning with its fires, its oaths, its recklessness amid the ripening fruits
    strangles like a winepress, my latest anguish
And reason winnowed by the flight of words counts the rosary of my
    acts
My speech grafted on the branches of the future unleashes the lightning of
    calamities and pride with its seams of gold
The rasping of weeds that cannot perceive signs or my repetitive prayer or
    the waves of my throat or the bruises of my voice
                    Awakens my calling
The mutiny of passion eases the storm into my mouth
And light-headed air feeds the gums that attack my joy
Coolness itself faints and already the swaddling clothes of the sun
    reconstitute under our steps a sweaty erection, gladness in the body
And the peasant goes off with his friend the moon to sow seeds despite the
    wickedness of men
For levees of sadness have hemmed in his song
Shattered layers of time mute the oracles
The very wind has marked his beach with silenced drums and insect
    buzzing, and the thorns of thirst have pierced his prayer
But awakening among the charms of the morning and the exaltations of
    words
The uncertain eyelids of the morning
Pupils swaying with energy or sluggishness
The aristocratic acidity of shackled ancestors
Exiled from the breasts of the sun
In the bilges' murky clamor
Caught in the jaws of good and evil
Have chosen his heart and his voice to sing stars and feats of war
Arise cries the farm-bred instinct of letters and furrows
The might of language will defeat loneliness
Light-shy termites will shrink at your words
Pray commands an inchoate alphabet
The march of the senses will overcome stones and ravines
The five parts of the world rejoice in our manly recitals
The whole universe is enclosed in our bodies

Plants, animals, streams, spirits roll between our hands
And we are mercy, the dwelling place of celebrants of all ranks and every sect
Stars winked and snickered
On the sidewalks of heaven twilight shook out its seditious rays
And the chorus of silence hesitated, faded
The deed of the plain is a blessing, for it watches over the town and its
    dreams
Day by day with a cup of water the lwas have examined the petitions of
    the abandoned and they have given sentence:
The event, so do we order, will start down the road

The peasant, head shaven, a thicker blot in the evening's outline, bluer
    than an autumn night, more energetic than those legendary battalions
    of the great faiths, releases his store of prayers beneath the astonished
    acacias and his words crackle in the dawn light before the hut drenched
    in the moon's reflected brilliance
I ask to be flooded with splendor, gladness, happiness,
My sower's joy is to enrich the plain
Every ear of corn is a joy for Erzulie
May the beneficial flesh of the avocado take courage
Oranges sweet and bitter feed and cure
The meadow quivered under the flood
Spare us, O lwas, the hail of punishments
Spare us notaries and court hearings
Keep the town fleas from sucking our flesh
Let the earth of our sweat vibrate with the organ's fullness
And let the hillsides resound
To crack the bits that choke our fate
Against the destruction of surveyors
And the ruins of speculation
A whole corset of refuse menaces, like ravens, the gestures of desire
And gnaws at the crest of our virility
Strew our ways not with scales but with the smooth shell of harmony
Language will see to alliance

———

Erzulie: with several distinct avatars, the *vaudou* goddess of love and beauty

Kill the mercenaries, the pillagers, and make our life a swarm of love, like a jar of cool water to encourage the pilgrim, like a waterfall across the path of Ogoun

And let the fanfare of free men burst out like a mad explosion, like the Antillean dawn and the island league

Let dawn redden over the waters the wizards the fruits, for the glory and ecstasy of the living

The glowing ravines, purified mountains, proffered hillsides, trembling bushes, hedges decked out in flower, demand a reckoning of bones from all mercenaries, from all slaughterers

O gods of Africa, partial to great voyages, your tears have wet all the horizons, have overtopped the doors of heaven with the bitterest of breaths, and ever since the earth has run wild with the sour saliva of pain, the painful foam of wars and discord

O gods scorched by the crackling of alcohol

O gods immunized by terror and hunger

Where can I find the free path that honors you, the firm path that releases you?

Prayer to the Sun

And from villages given over to the lewdness of males, to the fermentation of wives, to the exhalation of auguries, I summon to the arena of hell the excess of grandiosity, I awaken the tropical bee, the star that watches over promises of rapture, the red sun, the sun ringed with storm peaks, like those horsemen who chew their rage in the trenches of their retreat

And I lend my lips to the sun's fury as it carves across windows and the clefts of cliffs, on walls and on the membranes of the firmament, on every person and every inspiration, the dreams of a nation of colossi

I embrace to my heart's content the first ringdove of the first season, the bailiff and assessor of ages and sages, I besiege it with my breath, I twin it to my blood and my sweat and I still the antlers of humility, the rumor of pride

But the ramparts of silence give way to the hissing of dreams

The weakening of faith disbands reason and the heart

And the smoothest termites and even the cinnamon trees insult the fishpond that arises where sleep meets the hips

Like invisible wounds that mock the gaze, a sudden feeling of shame, arising from unknown regions, rubs its memory against my recovered joy and its claws seek my ruin

But I no longer hear the vibration of the waves that drive against the orgasm of my pride

In the neighborhood of the star I pluck the evanescence of a truth, always unknown, destroyed the moment it is born, always on the march and always ready

For it's not a delusion of happiness to snatch from the threshold of twilight the flight of a frivolous meditation

How many have perished who thought their lives depended on the scolding of the real?

But I, born in the abundance of paradise, fill every pause with vertigo. Mastery and fervor will reign where a discreet folly has played.

Is it despair to expose one's body to the aroma of an idea?

In the rough bed of memory, among stones spotted with attrition and compromise, my eruptions of lucidity torture my moans and it's like returning to life when I breathe a sigh of tenderness, a wild wave of caresses

The sea, like a sentry on a pedestal, nameless in the attraction of stars and earth, the restless sea, hoarse under her moving dress, unfolds her lace, splays out her trembling hem, whipping her islets, her shield of ashes and sound, her mane of ivy and silver in the shady but brilliant silence of innocent sand

And praised be her fervor, her distant and near rumblings, the harmony of her roars, the vigor of her swells and waves

For the sweet valor of the sea deposits simples on our shores wherewith to cure all corruption

The sea, the ever-solitary sea prolonging a song of age of widowhood, rolling her slipknot of waves and abysses like a conqueror dashing together victories, men and borders

The jewel-adorned sea unrolls in her progress a sheet embroidered with sensuality

The shining sea, armed with salt and sap, counts her mysteries and mends memory with the ripe elegance of imperishable fruit

The miserly, gossipy sea takes in her elbow the bending of my bow and expels with her tumult blasts of lightning and fascination

And her generations cover continents and nations

The sea accords with the wild screams of the *houngan* at prayer

Glory to those bitter gods, their wills battered by wind and sea, their bodies carved by the waves' movement, their outline glimpsed in the dance of living water

O joy to partake in the pleasure of the sun, in the delegation of her powers to the gods of hillsides and earth

These gods erect in the mist and the breakers, over the world's quagmire, these extraordinary, infinite, imperfectible gods

These gods lurking in disgrace and dirt

These giant, dwarf gods, keepers of garden paths

These gods trim the manuring of the fields

These gods of the sea and the underworld

Tell me what song they have failed to write on my memory caught between here and elsewhere.

---

houngan: the officiant at a *vaudou* temple

These gods have drunk too much on our fences

Their hair reflects the wrinkles of time

Now they reassemble in the flames of the day, startled, in commotion

At the first breath of wind, Ogoun, dressed in white, his legs crossed, with his clay pipe, lost in his cloud of smoke voted for an evening of blood

And the respiration of his thought is an ode to the impatience of his sons

And his word is the weaving of our deliberations, the pure drink of the sun,

       Hurrah for the gods and the crazed sea of the palm tree's tuning fork!

       Hurrah for their blurred gurglings in the sand, for the tyrant of so many lives, for this aquarium of odors, for this artfully polished roughness

       A pig's hot blood smokes in a distant village

       And the wild bells of the Angelus sing us their lullaby

       And here's Agoué

       Agoué rolls blue lightning in his body

       He projects purple glare on the edge of twilight

       His foamy belt licks the gravel, the reefs

       His many-colored crest grabs the eye

       He lynches lucidity

       And memory quakes to recall the ages of the sea, the bitter tears, the old vital salt and the sap of stars

       And Agoué constitutes himself provost of the waves, his breath is the sailor's stout breath and he crisscrosses the plaza with huge gestures

       And no sea grape comes to follow his ebbing retreat

       Nor the fever of the beaches that his wake calms

       Nor the man in search of beauty that his vigor enchants

But the violence of his sons, which he has come to reawaken

A hearty trance for the men of Haiti, a roiling of memory for the men of the Antilles

A flood of energy in the social flux, a crackling of courage in the despondency of disasters

Friendship for all rioters

And arrows thoroughly soaked in manchineel juice, and cups of its milk
and bunches of its fruit and its foliage and flowers

Friendship to the shattered continents, to the islands gutted by scabious
pirates in the centuries of decay

Dawn is rising in the rivers and ponds for every desire of the rebels

Stabilizing the yaw of every living word

And Agoué banishes fear:

Life shall no longer wander to deserted shores, to the glint of sharks' teeth,
to the flames of altars whose lamps no longer bear my name, where are
found neither oars, nor sail, nor masts, nor the mists of my breath

Let my population of mollusks and fishes occupy the whole space of the
dance

For I am a gestating hurricane, I command the waves and wavelets, the
rollers and the gale, the transmutation of thunder, the moving nakedness,
the shrieking fire of alchemy

And the child's healthy joy leaps up in pursuit of his birth, of his childhood,
of his seasons of ease and disease

    Sadness, his lullaby

    Is it you who comes to wound and break his sleep?

    Or his dancer friend

    Ungraspable but present

    Or her specter that assails me?

    But do you know my body

    That her pomegranates burst

    Like a horn solo

    From morning to sunset

    Like a million trills

    In my head and my song

    I am nothing but rebellion

    My vacant rusty senses

    My threadbare mornings

    My sleep exhausted

---

manchineel: The manchineel tree (*Hippomane mancenilla*, in French *mancenillier*) resembles a
crab-apple tree, but all its parts are powerfully poisonous, even to the touch. André Chenier
alludes to it in his fragmentary epic poem *Amérique*.

By life this museum
This spinner of misery
Life whines like a mosquito
With a rosary in her hands
Her rustic tyrannies

Child of water and earth, at the height of suffering, when the moon can no longer decide for herself whether she will shine tomorrow evening on men or on ghosts, when bombs burn the planet and the sea fades away next to the killers, when the solitary star lends its gold to the bodies of destruction, to the lovers of detergent joys, we celebrate, shod with the vines of famine, crowned with thunderbolts and wings, the disturbing zeal of mud and the raw festivals of the seasons

Our life erected on two tropics, our thirst stretched between two tropics, our truth, cracked, gashed, and bled by crime, we shudder at the moment of words, trembling in the mist and fervor in the swooning sap of a legend
Black man! Listen. It's the knell of the sun
Which has shed its body
Extinguished its grandeur
Its rays a splash of blood
Its domain a swamp
It soars toward the mud! See
Its heat the shadow of a hoary
Aquarium this winter horizon
But it brings joy to the ice
It dreamt of warming
It has chilled everything
From our close-knit hair,
From those packed bubbles
From that crown rejoicing under the wind's bare hand
Surges a source of incantations and questions
Child of water and earth, when your eyes embraced the light for the rumor of your dreams and the bulbs of your pleasure, a torrent of thunder held your country fast
With rings of iron, the Bridegroom perfumed the hands of the Beloved
For he thought it a profitable match to exchange the frostbite of his tongue

for the deceits of the Bride

Now your pen and paper stutter as if clothed with storm and hurricane

Like a fairy raped upon a mulberry tree, like a girl lost in her animal cage

And like a force one strains to bend

But mole-like, books sleep wrapped in their darkness, protecting their dead
    secret for the gods guided by the dawn have woven a path which your
    ancestors know

    They aided the human mind

    Always sensitive, always anxious and responsive

    To the sulfur of suffering, the salt wells of sighs

    Diligent in loving the flesh, in sanctifying sweat

    Heedless of the murmur of words

    To save life and hearts

    In the endurance of insomniac demigods

But, black child, the north wind of the soul has snatched your innocence

Already it threatens the seasons of your body

    Like foliage at autumn's touch

    Life an alphabet mutilated by Satan

    Like a plant betrayed by its own roots

Words like rush, jasper, or jasmine can never convey the plant and its
    flowers, their tones and colors

Confederates of man and his hunger, of his music and his silence, of his
    mind and his soil, they burst into life, watchful and curly, eager to
    germinate in places of charm or of tears where the wave sings, the storm
    plays, and the breath sours

The world moves in magic, fire in secrets and language in uncertainty

Science, coming from the place of the word, takes vengeance on men

And all the books are mute

Your skin is black and Gutenberg is white

All beautiful skies are blue

But the old men have their heads in the clouds

This is a trap

The handkerchief of the sun unfolded, took on color, glowed like a dial, like
    the echo of a festival, like a crayfish shell

And gossip, stories, the breathing of the guests waited for the shadow to
    fall plumb

And others continued singing:
Sun come sign a truce
To measure life to our dreams
The seasons are wearing our bodies away
And even our fertilized fields
Our hands our essence are smashed
And our loves are exhausted
By lawyers greedy for gold
Pull out your machetes for us
On every shore and every sea
Where notaries are in a laughing mood
And remove your bayonets
All our boats are galleys
Give us the city chopped fine
Misery has burned our steps
Flocks, game, dogs without memory
Stand ready for their daily feeding
To lap up illusory meals
They crowd around the water trough
And when their females give birth
They slobber with open mouths and jaws
But this is the life of a whole people
Where hunger is the only project
Put them all to the sword
This country devours every seed
With a madman's composure
Consuming a ballad in flames
While from its throat drip tears

The Sun's Reply

Like a restless fire I wander over oceans, deserts, rivers, wild spaces and meadows

Darkness, my nurse, the nemesis of age and time, attends until my coming the maelstrom of flowers, leaves, yesterday's clothes

When the eyelids of fear presage purple mornings to come, I come forth crowned with veils of dawn

And I depart in the evening for the thoughtful mirror of twilit delights and agonies

At daybreak rocks, stones, ditches, ivy, vases, beehives, lean-tos, ponds, rooftops, limestone and branches take advantage of my flesh, of my blood

The whole earth should honor me the apostle of harvest

Me, the fertilizer of the mind

Me, the golden stairs of memory

Me, the lung of the seasons

The spur and the dart of chilly meadows

Me, the prince of buried provinces

The butcher and quilt of berries

The signature of hedgerows, the medal of every reign

Already witnesses to my name have awakened in the East.

And why should sowers protest when my raiding parties approach?

Blazing phosphorescence glows in the east in the vapors of sex, of reason and mystery, of water resting in the melon, of water standing in the cane

Your role is to protect the crown of the Antilles, the cutting obverse of my sword, your bodyguard, your blood guard

And light is not my path but the trace of my steps

Seasonal waters remember my voice

Winter woolens come from a furnace

The last stars, my eyebrows, my eyelids, glow like a coal in the furrows of the beaten track

A sky without calamities, a friendly cabin, a profuse season, this is what the peasant desires each morning

And his childhood still juicy with dawn is like an accursed cloakroom

Haiti, you used to step forward amid gems, rainbows, and bursts of flame
A heavy partner plucks away your years
Horns, clogs, vampires rob your home daily
And cockroaches like rats intensifying ugliness
Your valor scared and marred
And children on the straw glut themselves with garlic and millet
And line themselves with dregs of life
They even bless the links of their chains
Drunk on a mixture of quinine tea and pineapple peel
Haiti, you, the real shaman of the Antilles
The blossoming of gods eroded the air and the well-being of our times
fell apart in flames
You were no Bois Caïman, but a caiman of fire and water led by the
wind wherever my splendor unveiled the enemy
Arise Haiti
A sleeper breathes the breath of dreams
I am the flute of time in the folds of the azure sky
Created and uncreated, I, the helmsman of the world, am the cause and
the torch of fate. My rays denounce the nightmares of the territory, the ugly
crabs who despoil you
I have not yet grown tired of your apostasies
But you have dishonored your explosion of gods
The thought of Africa inhabited one huge, sad, solitary tree and sealed
the compact of your blood with the fever of the Antilles
Damballah of the Aradas: he has the roundness of letters, the curve of
words, the angle and the rectitude of letters, the twists and turns of texts.
Hasn't he spoken from his fortress to the Haitian giants at the climax of
activity, sitting next to his wife, Aida, holding council and taking counsel in
the sky and committing to the lightning his veiled messages?
But see those wounded mountains
You who drink the blood of the day
These nearly bare streambeds

Bois Caïman: site of the *vaudou* ceremony that is said to have touched off the Haitian Revolution in 1791

Damballah: a lwa originating among the Arada people of Dahomey, who embodies strength and fecundity and is often represented as a gray or green snake

And those hidden springs
Clear the path of weeds
Feed, O seasons, the wild beasts of my dreams
The instant is clothed in my joys and my tears
Fruits, branches, hives, birds beg all the thirsty trees, impatient,
bothered by the fountain of time, trembling from the challenge of the stars
Here I am as naked as anyone, adorned like the estuary of the
centuries, ripe as the borders of a wound
And my sandals will seal the marriage of time and the senses
And I condemn morganatic marriages like those between Vaudou,
Rome, and great political States
Like the wind stirred by a half-open fan and the river by a broken cliff
Your desires are epiphanies
Don't go prematurely into the valleys and thorn brakes fraying the
virile frond of innocence
If all men melt into mankind, all the continents will uphold you
Let your dreams be vibrating arrows, do not boil them to shreds
through hatred or disorder
Love the Aztec gods, the Indian gods, and the millions of divinities,
they have the power to cut through knots and saw apart shackles
They are at work everywhere
In the placid silence of the hills, in the refuge of the peaks
In the spidery rhythm of night and day
And trust in me: I will hand over the secret of liberation
I the feathering of seasons and the pleasure of trees
I the live flame that takes the new seed
I don't delve into your thoughts, I know them only too well
I want to elucidate your acts
Alliances of armed souls horrify your gods
And the gums of Rome jubilate
For these hateful storms
That smashed your household gods and buried them
Faithless Rome, Rome the roundhouse of charnel houses
Following the fan palms, took on an appearance of custard apple
In careless sermons

---

custard apple: *Annona reticulata* (*cachiman*), a fruit eaten and used as a drink

One Easter morning, cried a cathedral curate, everything blew up in the name of the tiara

Country people wearing ties as if at a masked ball

Lescot ignorant as a crusader

Was squatting as he scribbled regulations against bogeymen in an old catechism

Which he went to read crouching by a bishop's crook

Scotched by a sketch of bloody business

For Vaudou came out of Boukman's mouth

It can never die, it is now temple, kingdom, citadel

For it has velvet vestments purified by the language of its priests

Mud, fleas, nails have purged its faith

The churches will die but Vaudou will never die

And now let us spit out every cult of creatures, of books, of tribes, of taboos, of rebuses

Before dawn I already harbored a rebel's breath

Haiti, you have every right to the masses for the living and the dead, for Africa's broad daylight and the bare cheeks of the Old World

The smoke of exploitation and serfdom will fade away

Haiti, you tiny exploding thorn, you must breathe more widely

Do you remember the long journey of your children?

When they came from Gabon, from Cameroon,
                     from Senegal
                     from Guinea
                     from the plains of Nigritia
                     from all over the black land
Miles of land separated them
                     undeciphered land
                     virgin land
                     air

———

Élie Lescot: president of Haiti from 1941 to 1946; overthrown in a popular uprising

Dutty Boukman: a literate (hence, "Book Man") slave born in Jamaica, led the Bois Caïman ceremony

Nigritia: a name found in seventeenth- and eighteenth-century travel descriptions for the coast of Senegal

air
air
Gods and years separated them
    their private life
    their public life in the fields of the ocean and the plantation
    intimacy and the country
    decades of intimacy that the sea ghetto broke apart
    all the faith they had to ingest
    Everything separated them
They were locked down firmly side by side
And looked at each other
And they had power over life and death
In the same language without understanding each other
And they experienced hell, hell
Every cherished memory reawakened the sufferings in their flesh
Every cherished memory blotted out the past
Every cherished memory sent them back to the instant
    amputating childhood
        father
        mother
        land of their birth
Every cherished memory attacked remembrance
    questioned society and the brave scientists
Every cherished memory widened the wound
Every cherished memory shook the foundations of the world
    warped into a questioning
And memories tortured their reason and their reason for living
    and unreasonable reason
    and the knowledge of Columbus the great navigator
  Oh! Captain! Director of human massacres
        Assassin of my pulses
        Nightmare of this black man's eyelids
        Termite of my human roots
We traveled in thousands, back bent, ropes around the neck, chains
    around our ankles, eyes fixed on the bottom of the boat
And a taste of gall in our mouths, we thought of hell
Iron linking us two by two
Black bread for our mouths

. . . We departed, they took us away . . .
On the horizon: a white man
. . . In our core: a whiteness . . .
All around us: black men
O black man where is your beauty
In the time of slave ships you spat in the face of white men
You fought for your life
You shouted Long live liberty for your palaces
                              the palace of your eyes
                              the palace of your nostrils
                              the palace of your ears
                              the palace of your hands
You wanted to be sole proprietor of your five senses
Every time Las Casas said *in nomine patris et filii*
You grabbed your machete
You evaluated truth by the insecurity of whites
Black man, you were beautiful when you wouldn't give up on yourself
You were beautiful when you sought in yourself your reasons for living
The sleepless nights of drumming
The nights of drumming and sleeplessness
The time of great conspiracies
The time of white conspiracies by the masters of knowledge
The time when your spurts of gold drove the Old World wild
The time when your lungs defied the breathing of the sea,
          the sea beloved of navigators,
       the sea that enables capture and confiscation
                    The sea, the sea
Mother of civilizations, mother of every transplant
Mother of stars and monsters, of worry and of love
The time when your red and black eyes promised to Africa,
Your mother, your flesh: restitution for theft, absolution for rape,
And return to the sun and to your ebony womb
The time when the product of your hands paid for the voluptuous
    evenings and reckless spending of the marquises of Versailles
The time when the machinery of your muscles set turning and maintained
    the arsenals and shipyards
The time of your repressed countered desires

The time of awakening to unexpressed passions
The time of awareness of a drunken world, a world subjected to the frenzy
    of power which turned into a delirium of impotence
The time of drumming and sleeplessness
The time of sleeplessness and drumming
The time the time
The time of your own passion
The time of your compassion for mankind
The time of your youth's adaptation to the greenness of the Old World
All the gods were there
Gods of Vaudou and of Rome
True and false gods
Unvanquished gods, the flesh is too alert
                        the spirit too piratical
Gods of incense, gods of drumming
Gods who did battle in the tumult of the bilges, the roaring of the sea
Gods who crossed paths, gods who went your separate ways
Gods who doomed yourselves in an enormous uproar
        where everything was lost
        where everything was ruined
            Both the misfortune of being gods
            And the misfortune of being men
Great black man remember
Remember that it was words, sounds, and colors
That condemned you, burned you, assassinated you
Do you remember your victory
Do you remember the victory of calindas and of Negritude
Of real Negritude on Haiti's soil
Of the Negrism of wilderness caves where you charmed even the most
    untamable snakes?
Forget none of your past
Neither Negrism nor Negritude
If the world despises you don't be scandalized
And know that this harsh exclusion will preserve the race of your children

——————
calinda: a stick-fighting dance performed by slaves in Haiti and elsewhere in the region, comparable to Brazilian capoeira

from burnings and gallows
from striptease, from prostitution
And fight, great black man, not to live
    They live and are happy
    But for the light that must crown you
You go everywhere a bit player in the streets of Europe
                in Europe's films
A love of thunder has taken hold of you
A love of lightning
A love of white walls
A love of reason, a hatred of seasons
A love of calculation and reinforced concrete
A love of calculation and sexual techniques
A thousand recipes teach the art of love
What are your body your heart worth
Your body is only its counterpart in gold
Your heart an oxygen pump
Your soul, stolen away
Great black man with luminous teeth
Show your bull's-heart tongue
Reveal your flowering star-apple gums
Open your mouth wide
And show the world the scars left by the hooks of Catholicism,
    civilization, and Greek culture
And ask the wizards of technology, the imperialist princes, the heroic
    inventors of insecticide and homicide, creators and destroyers of gods
Why Auschwitz and Buchenwald, why Madagascar
Why Hiroshima, why the escalation
And why even their scientific works are so laced with negricide verbiage
In the predawn hours rinsed with well-being, the weight of centuries
    lessens my strength
And my legitimate song freed of all fear hails the mermaid of shipyards,
    the sun, the stripped initiate
I say honor to the ambassador of planets and ages, to the healer of the
    scars of our dreams and of unhatched offenses

---

bull's heart: another name for custard apple

star-apple: *Chrysophyllum cainito*

And I demand from the priests, my associates, the secret and power of
  restoring threadbare speech to ward off the exudation of terror and
  despair
And it's Petro, the agile, early-morning spirit, the two-handed man, the
  border man,
  the bewitcher and the proxy
  the red-eyed man
  the accuser and the defense
  Pitiless and Insatiable
  the man who can get things done this side and that side of purgatory
  the man who registered my prayer
And who at the top of his tree-toppling voice accuses
  the city, that arena of massacres
  peopled with trouserless thieves
          with crabs and sharks
  the capital of blessed teeth
  the gall of the Vatican and its ringworm observing
  the angels with their infinite reasons
And resuming in a voice that made the young trunks shake, he spoke to
  the accursed countryside:
Daughter of the tempest you will weave your happiness
With the fresh water of tuberoses
With those singing hips
Plowing under, scalding those charmers' songs
At the top of disheveled trees
At the peak of untidy mountains
My turbulent black woman
With wrinkled, tattered feet
Your singed, wondering pain
On the red pillow of cashew
Mumbling about the awakened Antilles
About mad, hollow-cheeked Guyana
About colored America without sin or flame
Armed with fire blood anger
As a kind of epigram to shatter the trance

Petro: a family of martial lwas specific to Haiti

My lady, you'll see figs and cacao trees
    Mango trees, gods, satans in the alleyway
Pistachios, avocados, banana trees fighting
        All twisted up in space
Angels and lambs will be soldiers for hire
        Rocks quicker than vipers
Scorpions chameleons eager partners
    Without resting place, life, or landmark
Will make their way to the sanctuary and beseech the *vaudou* gods
        Entreating even the gale of days
Crying famine crying misery seeking lard
    A drum on their necks at every crossroad
It will be the age of justice and we'll see the promised land
Even if your mother becomes bitter and your guardian angel pulls in his
    wings
Your head will overcome false victories, the scourge of malaria
Your fruits will grow everywhere, even in clay
Your movable roots adjust you to the world
Music will offer its hand
Your word will be a torch
Your coffee will awaken the senses
Your rum will sing like a flute
The breathing of dragons, of serpents, will beat tam-tam, play trumpet,
    ring out clarinet
But you must pray
Serve the gods before you drink
Water the altar every day
And life will be reborn
For blaspheming hymns from the throats of capital are lying diadems
Only songs born warm from our huts deserve to live
You will hiss the cloud and affiliated mob of murderers
Your lamp will hang from the stars of heaven
Sea, earth, flesh, and air quiver in my light
Your torch, your fire in my flank
Your light in my babblings
Your color my warmth will go from one end of the world to the other
In the company of gods to plague the Occident

Set on my blazing rays
For the time is come to decapitate the town
And to clothe the gall of your resentments in purple
The time is come to measure faith and to listen
It is time to give shape to patience, to sing
Let us purify our hands with leaf sap before approaching the sanctuary
And the garrison of doves and the ring of cupbearers will come to serve
    my word

      And the flowers began to sing
Haiti is glowing like a cat
Her breath and her rapture spread abroad
Her men and hillsides are already singing
Cinnamon and spices play
The seasons will cover our fields with flowers
Life will come back to our settlements
And we will refresh words
We are headed toward magic
A hand has enriched our soils
Giving us repose
Coals of syllables pure as soil
Zones of love verbal paths
The bass drum is about to speak Kreyòl
Everybody will have a halo
Haiti will live in the light
More delicious than mint
No more Bouqui, no more Malice
Our gods will hail the pact
No more guerrilla
When all the camels are gone
Haiti Antilles Quisqueya
Bound more tightly than a single branch
Will soon be sailing downwind
If all their grandchildren come together

––––––––

Bouqui and Malice: figures from Haitian folktales, the slow-witted dupe and the clever trick-
ster, respectively

Our lives will advance by leaps
Arise, attack
Bohio, Toussaint, morning winds,
Echoing noises, cardinal points,
Banish the wrinkles of our cares
Steer us clear of cliffs
When the happy day comes
Let happiness be our guide
On the ruins of the night and under the sands of our prayers, life planted
　　its fires
Among the trills and runs of birds and the sweat of our dreams, the sun's
　　forked limbs seeded the earth
And these presents satisfied reason in hiding because of the nightmares'
　　tumult
　　　reason scared of the dance of words
　　　reason terrified to make the heart glad
　　　reason stripped bare by the rib of seasons
　　　reason still dripping with dew
　　　　　　Following a single road
　　　　　　Master of a single word
　　　　　　Blocked reality
　　　　　　The real, source of obsession
　　　　　　And proposer of death
　　　　　　　　　Like a great harvester
On the cusp of life and death, night, as it pulls the shutters closed, sculpted
　　festoons on the drawn-out day
　　　　　　　From age to age
　　　　　　　Night troubled memory
　　　　　　　Disemboweled hope
　　　　　　　From father to son
　　　　　　　Night zombified man
　　　　　　　From day to day
　　　　　　　Night suffocated history
　　　　　　　In the life of every generation
　　　　　　　Fatigued to see the return of dawn

---

bohio: a thatched hut in the language of the original Taino inhabitants of Haiti, who referred to the island interchangeably as Ayiti (mountainous land), Quisqueya (mother of islands), or Bohio (place of thatched houses)

Night sowed the bitterness of recollection
Bewitched by her own movements
Night lay her breath on still-warm wounds
And extinguished the possibility of rebirth
All faith turned to cinders
From early dawn, the peasant's flesh shuddered in his jacket
The man stumbled from sheer despair
Among the words that grew and shone in him, suddenly the image of a
woman took over:
A black woman with an enchanted body, with an immortal sex
Mainspring of my joy
Lever of my nights
Broken rocks of my hope
Cracked prow of my kingdom
Mornings in bloom of my childhood
Your impassioned flanks shine in my hands
And your blessed womb gives out deathless light
Oh woman
Fruit of the hilltops, eternal home
Black woman I touch my skin furrowed by the wind, transformed by fire,
harvested by the lwas
And I shriek
And I ask whatever lives and moves
the air I stir
the paper I confide in
my understanding table
the pen my blood
for news of your seasons
In your midst you have kneaded the most immaculate bodies
You fled all the days of compromise
You sowed in barren ground suns and rivulets, flowering of arms and
abundance of energy
From the resounding borders of my cradle, in the docile gravity of your
luxuriant sanctuary, I spell out a question
What has become of your faith after the ships' mortgage?
What does your bellowing grotto have to say about the brothers'
disappearance?

My children are gone cries the black woman
They've left the mourning dress of solitude in my heart
Their breath is expended on the frozen poles
They suffer on every continent, trapped by violent ruses
They are innocent
I will multiply my children to renew the world
        I will make them powerful
        I will bring them together
        I will give them the planet for their inheritance
In their hands I will deposit the vineyards of the world to come
They are too weak now to be left alone
    too frail for the development of concrete and H-bombs
They are like rootless leaves
At night my sap rises toward them like prayers to heaven but the
   technology-besotted day burns me along the way
I reach my children
    when human rage has defeated the mind
    when the body refreshes itself in the harmony of dormant senses
    when the season of dreams begins
    when the screen of dreams unfolds its icy fires, its clouds and its
    sparks, the anger and the outrage of sovereign pain
Woman crouching in an accursed space
    licked by madness
    twisted by shame
Woman deprived of gaiety
Woman cut off from light
Mother of the world how do the pores of your body vibrate
           how does the timid flame of your love breathe
Black woman reason for my song
       field of my joy
       fountain of my words
       source of kisses and gifts
Memories unsettle my warmth
For away from you my heart has no footing
I've observed many men and women
I've encountered mothers of men but not a single source of love
I've met painted faces but not a single nest of tenderness

No chalice of beauty has appeared to my gaze
My patience has drunk all colors
But all simply murdered my thirst
I no longer count the trap-bearing groves
The pepper of my hair that restores the green of things has taken the color
    of snow
And when I sought humankind beneath the thickness of flesh I found an
    immense despair
Black woman
Your body puts satin and silk to shame
                  and the translucent clothing of the most beautiful butterflies
Its caresses are like tropical rain in spring
Love envies me my stay on your beaches
My hand wanders upon you like waves across the sea
Your legs disappear where fecundity murmurs
Like columns of light
They go straight to your deep heaven
Weaving in the shade of your thighs and flowered arms the bare secret of
    your fastness
Your legs guardians of my virility
Snake through my dreams
And illumine my nights on the tropics of your fort, the lawn of my faith
Your body doesn't know winter
It takes orders from your heart
And the seasons honor it

And the sun filled the day, awakened the folded mountain paths, barked
    on mud tombs, on leaves painted by his fervor and on arable ground
    transfixed every morning by the bounding of steps
The earth lying ravished and lewd beneath her parent
And the whistling of the sun distilled the juice of fruits, thickened the
    ardor of the sap and inspired the prophetess who reigned through
    incense and violence over all the excrescences of life
All the plants shuddered
The sapotillas babbled
The tamarinds offered passersby a sensual potion
Man forgot thirst

From village to village the mounted parade of the day brought joy

But fury attacked in shadow by a petition embarked on a new massacre

Standing water in the mud, sober like a malevolent army, gave itself up to murkiness and even the toad's saliva praised the sun

Sinkholes and swamps, ponds and mud puddles excited their venom against the beacon's light

And everything took on a false color at the sight of this celestial gourd, doctrines and liturgies, plagues and bullies, dunes, the breasts of mountains

Everything lived sumptuously, the slaps of water, croaking of frogs, murmurs of insects and rustling of freshwater snails, bog mussels, the whole swamp fauna, reeds and cattails, all the potentates of the muddy zones emerged from their lethargy, laboring in the rising sun

Brine channels procured salt, the salt ponds rejoiced to see the salt gatherer musing atop the heap

The unslaked sun gnawed his protégés

The fraternity of wind and rain balked the *houngan*'s trances

The anopheles in its excess filled the cemeteries

And all the creatures that grow mid the marshes, the mollusks, the reed clumps, the wood snipes and the woodcocks, the thorn clumps and the oystercatchers, wild ducks and shovelers embraced the yeast of the day

The turtledoves and swallows smoothed their feathers

The vultures and mosquitoes, all the disinherited rabble of the night took an interest in sorcery

And bats rested at the edge of the woods

The gall of a single wingbeat rose in households and woke the children to take the cows to the spring

Tubers, those swellings of the earth, waited for the strong arms, the French peas, Congo peas, red peas, and black peas burst into flower and asked for the hand of young girls

And the spoils of pleasure turned to ash

The captive fires of prayer were barely visible in this conflagration of light

Morning mist buried pain

Cawing crowds brought together at the bedside of a dying man the hands needed for gardening and village work

Surveyors, notaries, lawyers, and proxies sneered

The proprietor would have to contract out his land
The city folk weren't there to breathe freely
They wanted to drink deeply
With the law on their side, announced by official stamps, by a dream
  suggested by a *hounsi*'s conviction, their speeches will fill their pockets
  and the guts of the countryside will feel the result of these confiscations
The gods fed on the previous day's offerings
The divinities of Dahomey and Nigeria said nothing
But Agassou, Agaou, Linglessou, the freemason lwas, praised the *hounsis'*
  purple robes
Legba and Mawu, mighty gods, contemplated the dripping of the
  universe's wine over the grass and meditated on high and low seasons
Ogou Badagri, insubordinate as always, clutching sabers and flags, on
  a disciplined mule, glared at the mob, made magic gestures at the
  audience
He revivified the blood of men and his red eyes awaited a convulsion, for
  he was not there to obtain evasion, ovation, discussion, or division but
  to restore the whole memory of the people, the death of the old days,
  the redemption of houses and vegetation
And the lwas went this way and that haloed with superstitions, favoring
  plantings and destructions, queering the aim of criminals and rascals
They fostered revolt and encouraged discontent
They fed guava trees, custard apples and canebrakes, logwoods and
  manioc, mango trees, cacao trees, acacias, potatoes and peanuts,
  alcoholism and forced labor, madness and tuberculosis, frangipani and
  fragmented humanity, calamities and malaria, poverty and hunger
Light depopulates and strains passion
It cuts across niches, fetishes, and riches
It befriends fallow ground
It likes watching deer and colts
Scaffolds and men are its guardians
The Pharisee and the innovator, the hypocrite and the revolutionary, sand
  and dew, the temple and the tomb, the newborn and the old man, the
  flesh and the spirit leap to meet it
For light resides in men's eyes

---

logwood: *Heamatoxylon campechianum*, a tree used to procure a black dye

In the roots that plunge into the earth
It's the footstep and millet of life
Broken pots and *hounsis*, stones and snakes, cocks and goats, banks and
    beaches glisten at its coming
Oh! Great mirror factory of earth and man,
        jeweler of overworked anguish,
        madness of drifting flames,
        the songbook of the universe has bombarded the eyebrows of hope
And now the nightingale's glory, through leaves, comes to revivify the
    savor and ripe pomegranate of humor
Amid the bustling of shades
Amid a whole people of worries
Amid these dreams singed by desperation and misunderstanding
The bewitching fervor of palm fronds has reawakened the sociability of
    pleasure's victims and discounted the sun's slapping in the name of his
    vigilance and necessity
The astonishment of ecstasy and disgust, of veneration and libel has put
    straight the blindness of men, swept aside the culminating infidelity of
    twilight and the unctuous syntax of solar insemination
Then the peasant suspends his joy, rolling beauties and sins together on
    his doorstep
It's a basin of obsession and delight, of depression and rapture, of
    merriment and gaiety
Heedless of today's obverse and reverse, unconcerned for the faces of
    today and tomorrow, he grasps the balance of the system and names
    himself mausoleum of extravagance
Bract of innocence
Ram of night and day
And no one can guess the health of my sweat, my black bread soup
    breath, the bitterness of my belly, the vanishing of garlic, watercress,
    and manioc patties
And I say to my song:
        Up like a stallion's hooves
        In the fields and in my veins
        Like a reflection in the water, standing among the throats of cane
        Like a mosquito manifesto
        meeting in the marsh

A hymn to charm apostasy
    Like a rotting disaster in the clatter of prayer nights
    Cousinage with fleas and sleep
    In the schism of civism and life
    On the order of sharks and shamans
    Like the common plane of bees and flowers
My nighttime and morning song, muted by the lowing of banks, whinnies
    and my song haunted by sacred maracas raises its headdress with the
    double ax of the god Shango sculpting the lwas' splendor
And my brave speculations on truth, on stones, on plants surrounding
    the *assoto* drum harvest and mow, scythe and glean possessions and
    metamorphoses
And I prudently bring forth the gilding of my hope
For the shells of my dream harbored firewood
A wasp's nest occupied the willow basket of my woman and the handle
    knew nothing
She thought she was transporting magic spells, one black hen and one
    white, fertile eggs and fresh ones
Even the droning sorcerer had commanded the gris-gris
All the roads were on alert
Ambush would dry out the great houses
Our dragnets and surprise attacks would bring the nobles to their knees
    before our lands
The oil of my submerged rage would chop up the town's privileges
The ticktock of dawn preceded us
The smoking pig carcass before the lean-tos obliged us to be discreet
And it's something to see in the first flame of the day when the young
    shepherd's voice calls his flock before encountering the teacher already
    wishing the day were over and finding the mayor and the prefect
    fattened by the countryside's juices sitting in some village rum shop like
    a rain-battered layer of dust, like the dollar's peat assaulting the sense
    of smell

Shango: a deified Yoruba king, honored in many New World African religions

assoto: a tall drum used in *vaudou* ceremonies

And disorderly dawn dropped bulbs of early light on every leaf and every
    drop of dew
A frenzied brilliance of foam, fear, fruition, orchards, proclaimed the
    complicity of bad luck and cheap rum, rubble, ghosts and kings and
    wildly licked the armpits of the dark
The mob grew in the plain, fed the nights, commenced new litters at
    the rate of a mule fertilizing the path while carrying his master to the
    temple
But new flutes with bird throats carved from reed stems often softened the
    searing of yellowed dreams
Like a hermaphrodite planet spreading its song of festivity and sex, at the
    peak of its flowering, a virile, humid, hot song in the tropical hills
Like a plant unfolding its precincts, its pleats
And the man thought of land:

        Land where I grew up
        Land that nurtured me
        Land of passion and levitation
        Land in perpetual germination
        Pole of shadows and silence
        Layer disturbed by restless tubers
        Trunk of steaming ebony
        What plant has not made the rounds of your veins
        Winter does not shed on you its lumpy tears of malfeasance
        Spring never seizes you in an icy cloak
        For summer and fall light up in your flanks
        The magic of your leaves restores youth to language, the virtue of
your fruits and the temperament of the colors you show so abundantly
celebrate hope
        Your obsessive and profuse flowers assail the fasting senses, stir up
the glum age of earth, quicken human blood
        The role of spring is to open the gates of truth
                    to attack all the ports of reason
               to keep intact the investiture of the gift
        And Haiti's land, reflective and cheerful like a young girl, bastion of
mystery, watches over the hearts of men
        The land of Haiti illuminates festivals and sings the supremacy of joy

Coloring the night with generosity
And delight is born in this land of anguish and assumption
The peasant knows that the machete will bloody the wrongdoers
show the way to unknown tombs
reduce boots and helmets to cinders
forbid mourning
Which is why ever since Louverture and Dessalines the whole land
of Haiti is covered in flames of uneasiness
Haiti's light plows through all rapture
And the wild moon kneels on the night when excess holds court
The earth hums in every season
All dreams sing desire
Not a scar on this prodigious womb
Not an overdone color in this field of rainbows
Not an odor but clings to the nostrils
And her sons are captives of the country

The sight of a man from Haiti's soil
Taste compressed of freshness and charm
Hearing that has inherited the skills of the wind
Hand laden with the ocean's first fruits
All the Haitian senses are sprites, wind goddesses
Haiti's land pregnant with fermentations and with a brigade of breadfruit
trees has forbidden weeping
It's a land of nonsense where drought has no place to hide
where the coconut tree captivates even the living sea
It's a land of childbirth
Accommodating the poet and the arsonist
the pink and the acacia
Haiti puts side by side the Spanish lime tree and the mimosa
She marries the logwood and the sapotilla
sweet potato and mango

Spanish lime: *Melicoccus bijugatus*, called *kénépier* in French and genip, kinep, or quinepa in
English, a fruit-bearing member of the soapberry family

She kneads the dew and sculpts life in the incubator of hunger
         in the zombies' dwelling
Her palm trees embroider clouds and pay homage to the pleasure of the
    day
The buds of her coffee trees make the night bubble
Her sores bring fear to the foliage and flowers
         to the bark and the roots
         to the breast of a peasant woman and the body of an initiate
Dry Mountain, eternally in prayer, fortifies
Abruptly a dream snags the memory and peoples the voice with a word of
    deep humility on behalf of a plant
    Greetings, respect said man to the cornstalk
    The reddish pride of your gaze
    Your grains that inspire the garden
    More tightly packed than a children's choir
    Stupefy our rejoicing
    And captivate our birds
    With your prodigies and charms
    Pilfered from the sun
    Your lordly headdress fascinates
    As it undulates and changes color
    In daylight's flickering
    With beaded forehead and firm flesh you carve on hunger
    Like forerunners, these hieratic forms
    These solemn hybrids rejecting every past
    Radiant splendor, autonomous bodies I mean your bread your hands
    Thirst eagerness for the cottage our hearts our suspended lives
    Jounce the crest of unhappiness and be they great or small
    The mad city, avid, steps forward, uncontrollable
    Like a whirlwind to admire your body, wanting to seize your tokens
    Giant or miniature according to your provenance
    For the next planting season ignore the frosts, your enemies
    You fight for beauty for the bellies of your sons
    Against the brutal rainstorms laying waste the south
    And I say salutations, respect, to all grain-bearing plants, to all nature
    To millet defying the heavens' austerity
    With its sheath and its ligula, its glumes and its spikelets

To millet displaying before fate the great cost of living
To the milk of my childhood the excitement of birdcages
To the breasts of drought clustered savanna flowers
To its warm lodgings to its faded shoulders
To the fragmented ease of a muscle of a fasting heart
And I salute the wind that assists the stamen as well
Fertilizing the ovary and stigmata of the millet
Vigorous, even if the clouds' breath has whistled past the wildness of a
field in need of gestures, even if the absentminded storm has shaken the
countryside, childhood and resistance with its proud waters
Greetings to the ascetic stalks
For on the days of great famine
Greenish, smooth, pale flowers
Promise bread and flour
The great shrub of hot seasons
Mother of all flesh
Leaves us her possessions and her saliva
Scrupulously and without a sigh
It's manioc husk of pure water
Clothed with earthen cloth
When the sun is angry
Manioc is the evening's bread
And when rain peels the whole earth bare
Manioc tells of the candlestick

But yam must be saluted too
Yellow yams sticky or dry
The fresh yam, purer than soursop milk
Is part of our evenings
It's a loud climbing plant
And grows ardently
It clasps the trunks and climbs them
Or spreads across the terrain
Like a rainstorm on a hill
It develops bulblets even at the base of its stem
Living silently in heat and rain
Until one day she reveals a store of coolness to eradicate misery

With fascinating tubers
This plant is a great soldier
The oldest of warriors
The untamed side of our combats

In the day's floating sparks, the huts scattered around the mapou yawn
toward the attic of the sky
Mountains, plains, and hills lose their leafage every year
The heat has seared the pink buds of the dawn
And any coolness that the sun has spied instantly took on the red tint of
autumn
And the plain rustles like a snickering band of scoundrels, mocking
household gods and lwas, throwing aside the donkey bones entrusted
to them

In full sight of naked children
Playing with their sex
Hunting for round stones
Making mud pies
With urine and saliva

A black child has a thousand resources against nature, more than one
asset in his struggle with the seasons, and in his way of accepting a life
born of ashes and sunlight a strength and subtlety that put to shame the
fantasy of the forest
The black child shouts when there falls on his soft and smooth skin,
pure as spring water filtered by rocks, sunlight distilled by a watchmaker
The black child shouts and demands to replace the inconstant sun with
his own body, the body that illuminates his nights
He asks to have his eyes take the leadership of a world made blind by
the smoke of gold

In the lumpy early morning
A child lashes delirium
The landscapes of dream bleed
And resentment stands on its thousand legs
In this peeled early morning
The child plays hide-and-seek
Hide-and-seek with the sun

Hide-and-seek with poverty
Hide-and-seek with his wounds
Hide-and-seek with his smile
Hide-and-seek with his own shadow
He thirsts after broad daylight
He turns his back on night
He lays a trap for the sun
Under the breast of the gods
The great traveler's tree of the lwas
He will strike the sun a huge blow on the temple
He will tie a thick rope around hunger's neck
And hang it from the traveler's tree
To exterminate poverty
And save his smile
To spare his shadow
And astonish the heavens
For the child shares in a passion for the dawn
He wants to implant this passion in the blood of other men
                    on lost foreheads
                    among the grass roots
                    on every tree trunk
                    in the pores of all flesh
                    and on every face
And the child takes joy for a waltz
Like the ocean dancing with waves
Like sadness dancing with tears
Like thirst dancing with saliva
Under the armpits of the early day

With the enthusiasm of his senses
With the vigor of a wood pigeon
Despite the creaking of pain
Despite the rough skin of days
The child has wiped his tears away
And here he is like a lion tamer
Occupying the sun's place
In the plexus of the dawn

The black child tames his nightmares
Hunger and demons
Hunger and humiliation
Breadless days and sickness
Hunger, wrinkled life
Hunger, midwife of shadows
Buried life
And the child stirs the foam of life
In the petals of early morning

And the black child sweeps every ruin from his memory
He comes to an understanding with desire
And his song will lick hope
Hope hidden in the folds of the day
              in the root fibers of lightning
Hope lying in the light of dreams
              in the grains of silence
Hope coiled in the pupils of the eyes
And his speech enumerates scarlet flowers
Rising over disarmed projects
Reweaving perforated dawns
And the song gains momentum
In the sobs of the early dawn
But he dances with sweat on his brow
Barely veiled he undoes his belt
He tortures flesh by exposing his trunk
And words crowd in from every angle
As if life were a carnival
As if life were magic
A rhythm of impudence
O gods O heavens
In the pulsation of the dawn
Your mouths are an orchard
Where waves live
Where a pastoral finds its people
In this bare early morning without rosebushes and without perfume
The mother takes her place inside her son to drink his tears

She will teach him to love
So as to weep in his place
To leave him her whole power of joy
And the tracks worn in her cheeks glisten
And the mother hesitates before the chapel
She tears asunder spiderwebs
In the marrow of the dawn

I've never seen her cheerful, this mother with bushy hair
I've never seen laughter cross her hollow-cheeked face
I've never spied her mouth uncovering the teeth that were the light
of her nights
When this mother told me the state of siege surrounding her
husband's fate
When she told me her son's nightmares, the emptiness of their larder
When she raised her arms toward heaven to implore once more the
grace of God
Tears came in floods
The eyes evaporated
The nostrils quivered
And her voice broke
When the children went to bed at ten in the morning despite spring's
deployment of all its beauties, fruits and diamond
When the youngest had neither shirt nor trousers to play in
When the second child could be clean only by awaiting the effect of
sunshine on the cherry branches
Tears came in floods
When the tireless beauty of a mother tanned by life must flee the
crowd because of the milk bill and the bakery note
When, shining even more brightly, her eyes skewered every passer-
by in order to avoid a meeting and bypass a creditor
When she came back with empty bottles and corn without oil for her
husband and her children
All the water in her body flowed

And at dawn with her poor provisions and her reed baskets
She waded toward the market

More heavy-laden than a mule
More rapid than an arrow
More agile than a goat
She mounted the slopes left bare by cyclones and deforestation
She slid down paths with indifference
The indifference with which memory exhumed in a dream the
infectious effluvia of time

And the father reckoned the profits of the convoy
Showing gums as uneven as a charred fruit
A mouth split like a peeled tree
Announcing his wish for the rainy season
When the pipirite sang his voice ran aground
For his jacket is as old as his son
Both of them ten years old
Life caresses and ripens children
Sweat and seasons rot his clothing
Like sea-foam rolling in to blot the horizon and wreck his rest
From first light on the swarming of poverty washes out dreams
And on all the paths the Haitian countryside engenders a huge
salivation of women
Hillsides flooded with colored kerchiefs exert a pull on rivers
Everything resonates with the worry of these market ladies
And a burning intake of hope like a shiver of dew in the shadow of
foliage crosses the spine
And the melancholy marketplace is blessed by the priest
Customers wander without buying
Thieves take advantage of a scuffle
And black women let loose their load of insults
They unload their wares
They call on the saints and the lwas
Policemen like insects use their antennae to break up arguments
In the heat of the early day

And men come to the market too
With a calf or a pig
They have called on Ogoun, they have drunk

They have examined their faces in every spring
They refreshed themselves
They have lit their pipes
In the mirror of the early day

And they walk around the market trailed by their livestock and
smiling at the girls they meet
And their sons topped with a stack of hats in palm leaf or sisal walk
around too
Milk runs from their noses at the sight of a girl

And I remember that woman and her child dressed in calico
That painfully beautiful peasant woman with her forehead polished
by rain and night chill

Forehead washed by the sun
This perfection of flesh
Body of sap
Supple like a waving reed
That woman more fragrant than a fruit peel
Despite the climb to reach the town
Despite the day no longer fresh
I remember that woman with her half-buttoned dress
That woman with her humiliated smile
That woman of ebony and ivory
That woman shouted "Pillage" to say she was selling her subsistence
And a thousand flames leapt from her mouth
A thousand candles shone in her eyes
And her voice cracked the passersby
Pride knelt at her feet
This woman burned by life shamed the pride of that town
But evening and night's approach showed her a path of red
The very market lay in silence
The peasant women cursed the town
They started back to their huts
In the odor of lemon trees and coffee trees
Horse urine and manure announced the countryside

And they all thought of the district officer, the tax collector
They took a brief drink at the springs by the road
A ruckus had erupted in the hedges, torn away the dew, freed the grasses, stunned will and desire
The houses had disrupted the road like an avalanche
The women's armpits
The babies in wrapping cloths
The body's every surface
The red rag of desire
Yesterday a slave, now a rebel Boukman, the rough peasant
Clung furiously to life
A flocculation of beauties with the plump ingenue quality of incapability suffocated bitterly in airtight accounts
These effervescent slices of existence had sunk into brutishness
Despite the lwas' shout to stop
Despite the predictions of a *hounsi*
Despite the breath of a *houngan* soaked in the breeze of truth
A hope armed by tension had uprooted the very essence of violence
The earth ground her entrails to bits
She reinvigorated roots for the genip tree's benefit
The yeast of green plains had stoned the crust of anxiety
The mountain, glad of her swellings, shattered the prisons, cast light into the chest of the country
The germination of red earth
The zone of spiny deserts, the forward pulse of clear streams,
Noon dreaming and staring over enchanted waters
All tormented the digestion of capital
Like a raging stream descending on a town
A roaring and baying stream sweeping away the magical foundations of spoils, shells, breastplates of power
The vanishing of splendor terrified despair
Unlettered peasant families, a tortured tropical crowd,
A turbulent wave of appetites like a dead wound
Emasculated the robber bands of profit and dispossession
Thighs and muscles packed the energy of the season into the glassy volcanic album of profiteers

In the terrific luxuriance of the elements
In the deep valleys of dependence
In the moaning of a bad awakening
In the infatuation of rootless legends
Facing a new implacable day
(O gods, light circles my shadow and my weaknesses
and noon approaches with rapid oars)
I don't need alcohol
Or tree bark
I'm stumbling already
The alleys, the street, and all kinds of evil spells have caught my
    attention
But it's living hell
It's Baron Samedi
Flee the moves of Lucifer
With his splendid prosternations
With his logical articulations
With his sublime funerals
Flee this poisonous bright day
Flee this trap-bearing date tree
I say courage to the man who sings
Courage to the man who fights
To the palm trees of the early morning
To the friends of our great traveler's tree

A knot of drunken light emerged with the eyes' opening
But fear came, exuding nightmare
The stems of joy wept
Fog's eyebrow flogged vision
At dawn's ticktock
Ambushes of charm discharged their venom
In dream-rusted close-curled hair
The stench of the town's overlords
Like a coral reef defied the uplands

Baron Samedi: in Vaudou lore, the guardian of the cemetery. Papa Doc was thought to have adopted some of his mannerisms of dress and speech.

Backed up against the sea
Fascinated by the great foreign castes
The country's riches shone forth like a ripe fruit
At dawn's ticktock
Animal madness drinks at the earth's wounds
Bloody coves opened on the sea
The mystery of brutality rules ports where posters of masked
    crocodiles glitter
Where live the drainers of all the earth's gold
The propertied class has Haiti nailed down
And waves seem to object
To flayings of flesh at ease with its shadow
To martyrdom, drill bits, stigmata, contusions
To this marshmallowy taste of sleepless toads

The sea turned all the luxurious nets into a slotted spoon
For human serpents burst forth on all sides
Sneering like minerals at the harvest
Like termites in the bottom of a basket

At the first ticktock of dawn
A nightmare's slap blended this fountain of men
Voices chants dances sank underground in the sparkling of day
A volley of prayers implored the tarnished stars
Abandoned to the wind, to waves, the terraces of time obeyed like the
    winking of one word the shrieks of a raving dollar
The hours shook off their past
The butterfly, his chrysalis
Man tossed away all memory
But the spark of rest engendered fetishism
A spell quickened the lean-tos and drifting palaces

At dawn's first ticktock
Amid mixed purples of discomfort
The goat's horn exhaled his patience in clotted lands
Tossed and haunted by violence, men
Sang the joy of renascent dust

They hailed the foaming of sadness on every sprig of hope
Tedium with its mists, silence with its limbo
The humors of urban pestilence
Enlivened the seasons' acid edges
Discreet palms of men pinned to the abscesses of life
Plucked courage bare
And let anxiety ooze forth

At dawn's first ticktock
The clouds' redemption has filled birds with musical gaiety
But veined with shadows and insults, the heart hemmed in by shades and
    arrows coated dawn's temples with rust
The mind's juicy flesh lay stretched out and raving
Like a flame rendered pale by glassy day
Disgust and volutes of loneliness had broken down all hope
A sad song breathed through the country mad for promises
And a very old dream cracked reason's asylum
Under the arbor the urban delegates evaluated saffron, vetiver, coffee, and
    the fidelity of the countryside
And the village women went to town to throw a season's energy, alive, dirt
    cheap, into some exporter's reserves

When the pipirite sings the sweat-crowned man sponges away his visions'
    madness and rage
With an ax and patience he has held off hunger and burned away
    nightmares
With the soles of his feet he has caused hope to rise over desert hills and
    galleries of earthworms
With the calluses of his hands he has threshed out his life, his joys and
    terrors, his future and his dead
In a coffee tree's shadow he has charred his last troubles and embraced
    dawn, his luminous lover, rootless lover, punctual and joyous lover, for
    a new start

When the pipirite sings the man in whom a new promise dwells
                    the man washed by the returning tide of day,
                    polished by silence

the man fed on prayers, sheltered in words' shadow
the man of exile
the man of water and fire
the man from nowhere plunges
the horizon into considerable bewilderment

When the pipirite sings the country summons me and I go down to hear
its murmurings and silences
And it's with a cry of wandering ripened in hostility that the new day's
shutters open

Among the incoherences left by sleep
Among the tranquility of softness
The early morning's mood sharpened
And he laughed at all those breaths without a home
at the builders' travels
at virile cults that are denied
at all those heads without a pillow
With the edge of his voice he insulted the bed of guile and rest
He shook prudence sitting on the threshold
He made limits rot
He denounced men curled up in the shadow of piety
who linked every work to tranquility
who attempted to construct under the auspices of peace
And his words woke me up
My memory was careful to consume all the dead leaves of lassitude
I set down in silence the weight of the world
And attentive to every spectacle
Watching for any gesture or sign
Perceiving the stirring of the most fragile desires
My senses were opened to wisdom and folly
Standing on the ledge of the day
I listened

The sun modulated his voice
The star trilled at daybreak

And I observed his luminous volleys on wicker and clay
Among songs rolling rusted in salt ponds
And ballads frozen by the foam and resin of words

Like the seasons contemplating the growth and the fall of trees I too, amid
    the noise, was part of the distraction of the alphabet
I listened to the words' wounds and complaining
And rebuilt the spirits' monument in a trice
Wayfarer of words, I blessed their ashes with my breath and my saliva,
    with my prayers and my hands
And abruptly the letters, grown wild like processions of bread trees,
    regained faith and began rustling, flittering, rambling like a lwa-
    possessed tribe
And in this tribe's keeping my mind forgot every other way
For in a foreign land, through the words that held me as a prisoner there, I
    knew my home and the voice that said:
    "Here sacrifices cease and miracles begin
    Here light begins and misery ends
    Stars hide in their own eyelids, words in their own echo
    And thus it is that the greatest mysteries become clear
    Let your speech stayed by faith misguide none
    And so stand as foundation"

And by the mouths of lwas words urged each other to discourse,
    domination, healing, revolution
Caped with colors, surrounded by hanging vines, naked, alive at last, they
    displayed the secrets of men, they dug out tumultuous alluvia of memory
        "In the hell-heat of your retreat, you crimsoned tombstones, the
        memory of bilges and iron has stained all your desires
        Decades of sinecure have weakened your heart, your vision, and
        made your breath waver
        Your loneliness is not yet too pure
        For see yourself sweating and soaked with centuries of error all
            around you, victim of reminiscence, helpless before Columbian
            plunder, capital's effrontery and hangmen's speculations
        Here begins dissent, here ends harmony
        Here ends concord, here begins knowledge

Accept at last the birth of one great vegetative blast, and the spread
of knowledge over all the leaves and up to the highest treetops
Because life is in singing
And your country abandoned to history's shallows is without
memory
As a liberation suddenly comes to mock the senses, so the nightmare of
the ages tracks our reason into its surest fastnesses
So now these dewpoints of time-bound deceptions, these Christocolian
fibberies come blurring vision
The hand must order its fingers
The country, reshape its sons
And wash its depraved flesh
And straighten bended knees
And deliver strangled voices
Wake its zombies
And brighten faded eyes
Reopen its psalm book
And regain self-mastery"
When the pipirite sings the voice that aided me through night and sleep
willed to the sun the tale of my desires
And a great mapou that watches my words' destiny marked the story's
bearings and hiked up its leaves to weave in its body the juice of my
dreams and put forward the hope tattooed on my heart
And my surexhausted breath sowed pompous nuggets of coquetry,
disorder, and joy

As the predawn rapture counted its insects, birds, and trees a very old ram
stroked the bare tracks of a hillside and his beard seemed to nourish the
new day's calm wind
And the town has already stripped the countryside bare, pillaged cellars,
attics, workshops and even the knots of the roots, leaving the branches
of the Gosseline River quite bare
And in this dancing day, O gods, O lwas, my word grows cool
The wind tears away my words
And I say courage to this early morning where the pollen of my dreams
dissipates
where the harvest of the sunset snakes away

to this early morning that nurses my roots
to this early morning without a name, without a past, without a future
to this early morning scarred by the force of the night
to this early morning lulled by my melody alone
to this early morning my obsession
to this early morning my hill
               my nest
               and my mirror
courage to this early morning my profile and my stream
                       my soil and my breath
                       my smooth contour and my sigh
                       my harvest and my barn
courage to this early morning my anxious province and my hay-cutting
    rhythm
                       my peaceful rapture and my
                         gaiety on great days
      to this early morning the spark of my song
      to this early morning the fire of my seasons
            the flowering branch of my sojourns
When the pipirite sings the glory of dawn has awakened every outrage
With the sword of daybreak I draw stairs along my path
    I brandish the dazzling bow of great internal legends
    I bless every bush and I wipe out the nests of anger

And madness is only a caprice of the memory of slave ships
All unawares I survey the opulence and the funerals of imagination
    false paths and misfortunes of enthusiasm
    the torments and turnings of great enterprises

And I return to peck in the field of words for daring
    and bells for stamping time
    time for shadows and butchery
    time for shells and sobs
    time for exploits and zombies
    this worn, pocked time
    this bent, torn time
    this time of fists

time of blood
time of bombs and famine
And I say courage to my receptacle-ears
For all the words that recall my time on the sea
For all the words that recall my time on land
For all those painted polite words
Those polished words
Words like "wax" and "couch"
Words that come alive before my eyes
Words ringing in my head
Words that roll deafly
Panting shameless words
Impaled speeding words
For every word that is spoken
I say courage to this early morning edged with green
    to the ease of this sleepless early morning
    to this early morning breathing among nightingale songs, the armpits
       of naked men and the taste of trees
    to this early morning already shaken by fate and the heavens rife
       with signs
    to this early morning thrown into the skiff of new times

When the pipirite sings I thread my way with words in the lapel of my
   hopes
Generously I assign landmarks to the folds of my faces
And I diligently sew together my disemboweled joys
      bandage the remorse of clumsy gods
      charm impatient crows
      wear out the coffins that seek desolation

When the pipirite sings I take a census of ashes, bones, and life
When the pipirite sings the world's buzzing comes to lash my sleep and
   my breathing
When the pipirite sings to the sun's summons, to the memory of my
   stained lips, I say faith and reverence to this early light compassed by
   my eyes

For a foretaste of dawn flows from the East's mane imitating the rainbow
For my pen manipulates the cunning of memory
    in the iridescent sadness of half-light's untanglings
For my speech preserves fuses of light in shy azure
All those constellations of malaise, regrets, stains, and ashes are
    condemned by my steps
And the dominance of dawn foretells treasures and gaiety, the day's
    sadness and accumulated dust, the presence of those chains knotted by
    centuries, chains forged for the purpose of inflaming life
And garrulous dawn makes us shiver like a merry-go-round spinning for
    the children's greater joy
For the touch of half-light has raised the dead
And out of those scurvy, snarling images sprang (as if from a beautiful
    unknown language) shining figures of conquest
And reason yields once more to the guidance of the word

In the rock quarry of words is loudly born a dashing collection of zombies
    who reveal the hidden side of millennia of deception
The urns of time have cajoled their now tender, wild, and prophetic womb
And memory dressed in stars still signs with a flourish across the wound
    of oblivion
Intrepid she rushes to all fronts, reviving despair
But day, compass-blessed day
Day brisk and sharp-winded
Day startled the pith of suffering as it burst in leafy dew, wingbeats, and
    cock-a-doodles
And our digging disturbs health, the daring and rituals of life

When the pipirite sings nakedness takes hold of the senses
Dawn wakens every thorn
Still yellow from her dreams, dawn hurried and naked
Delights in her birth and confirms me alive
And in the early light human specters, the work of fear, double and
    redouble
In dawn's coals I replant my childhood's magnetic hope, renewed ruins of
    desire, the seed of violence peeled bare

When the pipirite sings, knowingly, with salt and water I set out a spirit
    path
In my own measure, with rum and fire, I set the gall of doctrines alight,
    inflame history's skies
With my breath and my blood, my roots, my intestines, I warn a
    glowing substance against trickery and my tongue exacerbates social
    transgressions

When the pipirite sings I wash away, with the fresh water of my dreams,
    grave proclamations sprung from the shores of profit
And what I say, bound up with my source, gags the foaming of all
    extrinsic waters—all decorous cries—and shod in irreverence tramples
    the hubbub of all foreign words

Métellus offers the following footnote on the title of the poem: "In Haiti, the *pipirite* is the first
bird one hears singing in the morning, a little like the lark in European climates." The pipir-
ite's name derives from its call. *Au pipirite chantant*, the title of the present long poem and of
the book in which it appears, is a colloquial Haitian phrase meaning "at daybreak." The poem
was first published in the journal *Les lettres nouvelles* in 1973. Its recurrent refrains "When the
pipirite sings" and "At dawn's first ticktock" echo and challenge the refrain of Aimé Césaire's
epochal *Cahier d'un retour au pays natal*, "Au bout du petit matin" (translated as "at the end of
first light" by A. James Arnold and Clayton Eshleman in Césaire, *The Original 1939 Notebook
of a Return to the Native Land* [Middletown, Conn.: Wesleyan University Press, 2013], 3).

No Reprieve

No reprieve for the man steeped in the word
For life rolls and howls
Crazier than death's embrace
More fevered than the eyelashes of the sun
Life might come tomorrow vaulting into my hut
To chase away the pain caked on my skin
Light up my shipwrecked cot
Make me forget my cradle of rain
And all the rippling banks of my nights
And all the rheumy sweep of glances
But the earth, the earth, the earth I worked yesterday
The earth still stuck to my face
The dirt I plowed
Went off with the last downpour
Carrying songs and seed into the sea
And now not even a caterpillar would willingly live under my feet
The fields' teeth have chewed at my patience
And my breath is as fragile as a flower

(Au pipirite chantant, 1978)

Land

I am the one shore in the memory of the Antilles
And the delectable cheek which radiates and welcomes fragrance
I am the generous lips of childhood
Haiti, Quisqueya, Bohio,
Land both welcoming and cool
I wanted to clamp you living in my arms,
Build you a monument of organs and flutes,
People you with incense and celebrations,
Revive your off-seasons,
Adorn your houses' trim
Eldest daughter of the Antilles,
You've seen your children die
You've drunk the blood of hurricanes
As paper drinks the ink from my pen
As the land drinks its mother's sweat
As the trespasser drinks your milk's essence
As fire drinks a season's gold
As a sharp-edged blade drinks a life's story
Do you know the names of the locusts that have stripped your orchards?
And the source of the scum that floats like the toad's drool
Across your withered body slashed from head to toe
No longer can I see those piercing eyes of yours which used to trap
    fragrance, happiness
And subdue the snake
Yet still do you eat cinnamon whole, calyx, seedpod, and all

Drink raw eggs with gusto
Eat whole cloves of garlic
For the great pleasure of your entrails and the protection of your beauty
And what do you do with wormwood which casts out evil spirits' spells

(*Voyance*, 1985)

Death in Haiti

Somewhere on this earth a King who wears his Sunday best seven days a week twenty-four hours a day goes around in the guise of everybody's desires.

Nowhere will a living creature be better received.

Nowhere do the Cyclones, Storms, and Tempests find a better terrain, better exert their power, sing more loudly, carry off more children in their arms, find so many shacks or so much life to fill up the waters rolling night and day.

A king who wears his Sunday best whose job is to deal with everything including the human heart and the roots of trees gets ready his share of surprise for every power alongside his work.

Nowhere in the world is the child more fragile, the mother more burdened.

Nowhere in the world do the jaws of the earth find fresher meat.

Nowhere do the graveyards suck up more children.

Everywhere in Haiti, in the Haitian milieu, the hours give the shivers to every living soul.

Only the child plays in the face of nature and trembles at the power of things, inhabited by death who uproots here and there steals away a girl, a bush, the hopes of a region, the proud passions of a couple, the very point of living.

If you're a peasant you don't go to school. Starting at three in the morning when the moon shines brightest the five-year-old child goes on a seven-mile walk to graze his animals on a great-uncle's patch of land.

During these rambles which give him real muscles and powerful lungs, broken bottle glass pumps away his blood to fatten the earth where the tetanus bacteria thrives.

And the father on his horse studies the plantings

> the children
> looks at heaven and earth

the eternal seasons of the heart and body
the only trustworthy mirrors of man
the only meditation sites
But the signs of earth are not predicting abundance
And heaven's signals are for the initiates alone

We're a long way from Africa, the father thinks,
a long way from Africa
where the gods attended our ceremonies in person
where the gods blasted the hiding places of death by the
mere breathing of their will, by a single yes to our prayers
a long way from that Africa where a tyrant knelt on hearing the mere
name of the gods

a long way from that Africa where everyone could sing and serve
the gods of water and love
the gods of earth and the hearth
the mystery gods who taught man the secret of the world, the
function of the heavenly lights, of the moon and the stars
a long way from that Africa where the gods gave strength to our
arms for no purpose but to bring back to the village a fine boar for the
feast in honor of a newborn
Now in Haiti one father's arm is equipped to bring down another father
the brother kills his brother
the father attacks the son
and the mother endures
Blood flows every day at Port-au-Prince
life is sad in this great town
the president knows neither his father
nor his daughter
nor his son
He brings human blood to ceremonies instead of goat blood
he cuts life short
Life in Haiti from morning on lies flat like a noonday sun surprised by a
 cyclone

(*Au pipirite chantant*, 1978)

Words

My heart gives itself up to words
Confiding to them its distress

Come back, my courage
Come back in this season of abstinence and patience
In the middle of those hollow defenseless hours
Lift up my shoulders eyelids forehead
With everyday words, no flowers, no embellishments
Without those old sorrows, without those hellish memories
Without those grievous gestures and shameful affronts
Without veil, without insolence, without a frown
Without exaggeration, without change of heart
Come back, my courage, to live among words
And decode the long message rolling along the beach
In the elusive language of foam
In the salty rumbling that defies the ages
In sun, rain, or rainbow
Question those tireless implacable waves
Clothed in anger every season of the year

Oh to understand the movement that rocks the sand
And polishes stones

(Braises de la mémoire, 2009)

Ogoun

I am, said Ogoun
The mountain of mud, of evil, of curiosity
I wasn't just the god of Haiti's land
I was the god of her oceans
I was the magic
My mouth was your fountain, your universe
That war was no tournament
It whirled round every hut
When you came to see me
You staggered like sheep stricken with scabies
All those things you now tell as legends
Bore the stamp of your God!
Now I'm only a rumble from your past
I who turned your disasters into victories
I put an end to the blind perversity devouring you
To cruelties and cyclones humming with human blood
All the bullets that strayed into your bodies
I dug them out with my sword
I made you forget the ropes that once trussed you
And the ships where you fornicated in the urine and excrement
Maybe you miss the days when they flayed you alive
And you walked chained up and branded

Ogoun: one of the chief male gods of the *vaudou* pantheon, also known as Ogou, Maître Ogou, or Ogoun-Ferraille. Ogoun seems to have begun as a patron god of ironsmiths in West Africa. Being associated with iron and fire, he then took the position of a god of war.

And to think I rocked you under the tragic tropical sun
Back then the quarters were your breathing space
Your elbow room a huge pit
I had to sculpt your whipweals
And out of your peoples, your jumble of tribes
I fashioned a people with a future in its face
Too much talk irritates me
Hold up, hold up my struggling body
The air of my passion, the wings of my exploits
Still exalt my altar
Thankless sons
Give me GIVE ME the veneration I deserve
Moonshine, molasses, rum, a little lamb no longer suffice
Wait till you're rich to offer a bull, a candlestick
Like a tree dropping already insect-gnawed fruits

All insomnia is warlike
All insomnia is harsh and cruel

My footfalls have awakened bats
On paths weaned of the rainbow's flame
I was on my way to question the stalk of a tortured vine
The leaves' dry and mournful noise made a leaky roof
Through which saffron lights came whispering the torments of hell
My eyes scraped, dug portholes in the night
I spun prayers attended by drizzle
Down in those vast chasms of hope
And down in a heart scented with insomniac shudders
And my words came from far-off depths

(*Au pipirite chantant*, 1978)

The Wretched of This Life

The wretched of this life
Get around Paris in that freaky skin
Dessalines's grandsons, descendants of Zulu kings,
     outcasts of African empire, unbaptized,
     purebloods and mestizos, dispossessed,
     exiles from every quarter, undocumented, stout
     arms and wrecked lungs

The wretched of this life
Wear a black skin in winter lands they
Go along head lowered, a faraway look in their eyes,
     accursed mouth, broom under the arm, a
     pruning knife in hand, garbage bin on their heads,
     pack on their shoulders, and on their wrists
     the handcuffs of illusion

The wretched of this life
Live twelve months in a row with snow in their hearts
They live in the shadows of a City of Light

"The Wretched of This Life" cites the first verse of "The Internationale" and also Frantz Fanon's *Les damnés de la terre* (Paris: Maspero, 1961), translated by Constance Farrington as *The Wretched of the Earth* (New York: Grove Press, 1963). Fanon's analysis of internalized racism among black people powerfully affected Métellus in his student years, and Jean-Paul Sartre's preface to the work stimulated the as yet unknown student writer to submit his poems to Sartre's journal *Les Temps modernes*. See Françoise Siri, "Jean Métellus, et un jour le neurolinguiste devint poète," *L'Humanité*, January 7, 2014.

They go to work without tea, coffee, or bread,
      mouth frozen, tongue glued, throat
      big with a blocked sigh, a strangled wish

The wretched of this life
Are those pointed out in public
On their faces a painful smile
In their hearts a lava of burning misery

Those who don't know a single letter, can't even write
      their name, can't be found in the official
      registers but sign contracts and
      agree to work for a duration
unknown to them and a pittance

They bear the cross of the world

(Hommes de plein vent, 1992)

This poem is from *Hommes de plein vent* (Ivry-sur-Seine, Fr.: Éditions Nouvelles du Sud, 1992), 99–100; text slightly altered as in *Hommes de plein vent, hommes de plein ciel* (Paris: Éditions de Janus, 2011), 117–18.

For a Haitian Schoolboy

Child of water and earth growing up beneath the Tropics in the fiercest of seasons, when the moon can no longer decide for herself whether she will shine tomorrow evening on men or on bones, when the sun has confided to the most human of men its despair at laughing only for the killers with bombs and machine guns who head for the coast where the sea the earth the sun and the sand meet to tan their bodies and infuse their veins' water with the very salt of life,

child of water and earth subjecting to the morning fire of a tropical sun eyes chilled by hunger and notebook pages, eyes whitened by paper,

Child, child with hair knotted from your mother's belly onward into a thousand worries that will become your permanent companions,

Black child with peppercorn hair massing into battalions just so as to have a word to say in this whole dispute,

Extraordinary black child now enslaved by white paper, where is your truth, where is the teacher's truth? Where does he get what he's telling you? And for whom does the earth turn? What is this crazy story? What is this truth?

Your truths are not yet written. They are to be deciphered in day's recovery from night, from your body's weight, the sun's crystal, from all the shapes the moon takes, from earthly swamps.

Once upon a time, your very proud ancestors believed peace had been proclaimed when pens and paper burned, when schools were empty and churches closed, when palace walls blew up, now do you know where it can lead, this irrational need for a boy black from head to toe to go looking for the way and the truth in books that are not written for all men?

Are you sure you can see yourself in the well-traced paths that lead where men kill, are you sure you're not betraying your fathers, Dessalines and Toussaint, Christophe and Péralte, is it natural to love books and authors and all that sort of life that worships things on paper without always considering the flesh that suffers and waits, the heart that beats, eyes that laugh, hands formed for the wheel and the piano, fingers sculpted to hold a pen or a bunch of nails?

Black child, what trap have you fallen into? For here comes the mind's North Wind to rob you of your innocence and cut short the seasons of your body to make autumn leaves of you in the finest springtime of your alphabet.

Watch out, son, all the letters are in cahoots. The spirit is one, bodies are alike but humankind is diverse . . . It doesn't add up.

Keep that alphabet of yours firmly on top of your helmet of thorns. Twenty-six letters can never express a cockcrow; the leaves of trees, the colors of flowers, and the rumblings of a hungry belly only enter language in order to expose both numbers and dictionaries to the greatest ridicule, watch out.

The world is large, humans small, the universe incommensurable; neither matter nor infinity can explain a single falling hair, be careful.

A moving body has its magic, fire has its secrets as it burns, the tongue is all prepared to repeat, watch out.

Where does Science come from, anyway, where do we get the Word? Where does the world come from, where are people going? Don't be in a hurry to give book answers. Think carefully.

(*Au pipirite chantant*, 1978)

Jean-Jacques Dessalines, Toussaint Louverture, Henri Christophe, Charlemagne Péralte: heroes of the Haitian Revolution (1791–1804) and of the Cacos Rebellion (1916–1919)

ACKNOWLEDGMENTS

Jean Métellus and Anne-Marie Cercelet-Métellus have generously encouraged this project for years. I gratefully remember afternoons *en famille* under the arbor in Bonneuil-sur-Marne and a day spent talking at the Sorbonne with Michel Serres, Jean Bessière, and the poet.

My next greatest debt is to Paul Farmer, who introduced me to Haiti and Haitian poets. Some of the translations here were done in collaboration with him, but so long ago that I no longer know where to give credit. Françoise Lionnet and Jacob Edmond, by sharing their work and pointing out rough places in mine, have helped me recognize the challenges of translating a type of writing that, whatever its place of composition, builds on its relation to many local forms of language. The editorial enthusiasm of Jill Petty and Anne Gendler, combined with Mike Ashby's alertness to wording and the sharp eye of Iván Pérez-Zayas, has made the last stages of the project a pleasure.

I am grateful to *World Literature Today* for giving permission to republish the translations of "Words," "No Reprieve," and "Land" from *World Literature Today* 83, no. 4 (July–August 2009): 38–40. An earlier version of the foreword appeared as "Jean Métellus: A Portrait of the Artist as Horse," *Cambridge Literary Review* 3 (2010): 208–24; I thank the editors for kindly allowing republication.

Adamson, Ginette. "Jean Métellus: Insuffler une respiration jacmélienne à la mémoire haïtienne." In *Écrits d'Haïti: Perspectives sur la littérature haïtienne contemporaine (1986–2006)*, edited by Nadève Menard, 39–48. Paris: Karthala, 2011.

Bates, Thomas R. "Gramsci and the Theory of Hegemony." *Journal of the History of Ideas* 36, no. 2 (1975): 351–66.

Berrou, Raphaël, and Pradel Pompilus. *Histoire de la littérature haïtienne illustrée par les textes.* 3 vols. Port-au-Prince: Éditions Caraïbes, 1975–77.

Caroit, Jean-Michel. "Jean Métellus (1937–2014), figure de la scène intellectuelle haïtienne." *Le Monde,* January 15, 2014.

Césaire, Aimé. *Cahier d'un retour au pays natal.* 1939. Reprint, Paris: Présence Africaine, 1956. Translated by Anna Bostock and John Berger as *Return to My Native Land* (Baltimore: Penguin, 1969).

——. *The Original 1939 Notebook of a Return to the Native Land.* Translated by A. James Arnold and Clayton Eshleman. Middletown, Conn.: Wesleyan University Press, 2013.

Chenier, André. *Oeuvres complètes.* Edited by Paul Dimoff. Paris: Delagrave, 1920.

Dash, J. Michael. "Fictions of Displacement: Locating Modern Haitian Narratives." *Small Axe* 12, no. 3 (2008): 32–41.

——. "Haïti première république noire des lettres." *Littératures noires*, April 21, 2011. http://actesbranly.revues.org/480.

——. "Nineteenth-Century Haiti and the Archipelago of the Americas: Anténor Firmin's Letters from St. Thomas." *Research in African Literatures* 35, no. 2 (2004): 44–53.

Depestre, René. *Un arc-en-ciel pour l'occident chrétien: Poème-mystère vaudou.* Paris: Présence Africaine, 1967. Translated by Joan Dayan as *A Rain-*

bow for the Christian West (Amherst: University of Massachusetts Press, 1977).

Fanon, Frantz. *Les damnés de la terre*. Paris: Maspero, 1961. Translated by Constance Farrington as *The Wretched of the Earth* (New York: Grove Press, 1963).

Ferguson, Charles A. "Diglossia." *Word* 15, no. 2 (1959): 325–40.

Girard, Philippe R. "Quelle langue parlait Toussaint Louverture? Le mémoire du fort de Joux et les origines du kreyòl haïtien." *Annales* 68, no. 1 (2013): 109–32.

Hazlitt, William. *Lectures on the English Poets*. Oxford: Oxford University Press, 1952.

Jonassaint, Jean. *Le Pouvoir des mots, les mots du pouvoir*. Montreal: Presses de l'Université de Montréal, 1986.

Keats, John. *The Complete Poetical Works and Letters of John Keats*. Boston: Houghton Mifflin, 1899.

Lattimore, Richmond, trans. *The Iliad of Homer*. Chicago: University of Chicago Press, 1951.

"Le poète et neuro-linguiste haïtien Jean Métellus est mort." *L'Humanité*, January 6, 2014.

Métellus, Jean. *Anacaona*. Paris: Hatier, 1986.

——. "Analyse linguistique de corpus de langage d'aphasiques." Ph.D. diss., University of Paris III, 1975.

——. "Au pipirite chantant." *Les lettres nouvelles*, June–July 1973, 7–72.

——. *Au pipirite chantant: Poèmes*. Paris: Les Lettres Nouvelles, Maurice Nadeau, 1978.

——. *Braises de la mémoire*. Paris: Éditions de Janus, 2009.

——. *Charles-Honoré Bonnefoy*. Paris: Gallimard, 1990.

——. *Colomb*. Case-Pilote, Martinique: Autre mer, 1992.

——. *Éléments*. Paris: Éditions de Janus, 2008.

——. *Empreintes*. Paris: Éditions de Janus, 2013.

——. *Haïti, mon île exposée et secrète*. Paris: Éditions de Janus, 2015.

——. *Haïti: Une nation pathétique*. Paris: Denoël, 1987.

——. *Hommes de plein vent*. Ivry-sur-Seine, Fr.: Éditions Nouvelles du Sud, 1992.

——. *Hommes de plein vent, hommes de plein ciel*. Paris: Éditions de Janus, 2011.

——. *Jacmel au crépuscule*. Paris: Gallimard, 1981.

——. *Jacmel, toujours*. Paris: Éditions de Janus, 2007.

——. *Jean Métellus et le miroir du monde.* Paris: Éditions de Janus, 2015.

——. *La famille Vortex.* Paris: Gallimard, 1982.

——. *L'année Dessalines.* Paris: Gallimard, 1986.

——. *La parole prisonnière.* Paris: Gallimard, 1986.

——. *La peau et autres poèmes.* Paris: Seghers, 2006.

——. *L'Archevêque.* Pantin, Fr.: Le Temps des Cerises, 1999.

——. "L'automatisme et la volonté dans le langage de l'aphasique âgé." *Médecine et Hygiène* 35 (1977): 1961–65.

——. *La vie en partage.* Paris: Desclée de Brouwer, 2000.

——. *Le pont rouge.* Paris: Éditions Nouvelles du Sud, 1991.

——. *Les Cacos.* Paris: Gallimard, 1989.

——. *Les dieux pèlerins.* Ivry-sur-Seine, Fr.: Éditions Nouvelles du Sud, 1997.

——. *Louis Vortex.* Paris: Messidor, 1992.

——. "Marcel Jousse et l'anthropologie du geste." *Nouvelle revue française* 332 (1980): 60–67.

——. *Rhapsodie pour Hispaniola.* Paris: Doucey, 2015.

——. *Toussaint Louverture, ou Les racines de la liberté: Théâtre.* Paris: Hatier, 2003.

——. *Une eau-forte.* Paris: Gallimard, 1983.

———. *Voix nègres, voix rebelles.* Pantin, Fr.: Le Temps des Cerises, 2000.

——. *The Vortex Family.* Translated by Michael Richardson. London: Owen, 1995.

——. *Voyage à travers le langage.* Isbergues, Fr.: Ortho-Édition, 1996.

——. *Voyance.* Paris: Hatier, 1984.

Métellus, Jean, and Marcel Dorigny. *De l'esclavage aux abolitions: XVIIIe–XXe siècles.* Paris: Cercle d'art, 1998.

Métellus, Jean, and Jacques-Hubert de Poncheville. *Sous la dictée du vrai.* Paris: Desclée de Brouwer, 1999.

Métellus, Jean, and Béatrice Sauvageot. *Vive la dyslexie!* Paris: Nil, 2002.

Métraux, Alfred. *Le vaudou haïtien.* Paris: Gallimard, 1958.

Pollock, Sheldon. *The Language of the Gods in the World of Men: Sanskrit, Culture, and Power in Premodern India.* Berkeley: University of California Press, 2006.

Prevallet, Kristin, trans. "Two Poems by Jean Métellus." *BOMB* 90 (Winter 2005). http://bombmagazine.org/article/2701/two-poems.

Price-Mars, Jean. *Ainsi parla l'Oncle: essais d'ethnographie.* Port-au-Prince: Chenet, 1928.

———. *Ainsi parla l'Oncle suivi de Revisiter l'Oncle*. Montreal: Mémoire d'encrier, 2009.

———. *La vocation de l'élite*. Port-au-Prince: Chenet, 1919.

Saussy, Haun. "A Note on René Bélance" and "Fourteen Poems by René Bélance." *Callaloo* 22, no. 2 (1999): 351–62.

Siri, Françoise. "Jean Métellus, et un jour le neurolinguiste devint poète." *L'Humanité*, January 7, 2014.